Epistemological, Ethical and Political Issues in Modern Philosophy

Eray Yağanak / Ahmet Umut Hacıfevzioğlu (eds.)

Epistemological, Ethical and Political Issues in Modern Philosophy

PETER LANG

Bibliographic Information published by the Deutsche Nationalbibliothek
The Deutsche Nationalbibliothek lists this publication in the Deutsche
Nationalbibliografie; detailed bibliographic data is available online
at http://dnb.d-nb.de.

Library of Congress Cataloging-in-Publication Data
A CIP catalog record for this book has been applied for at the Library of Congress.

Cover image: iStock.com/firebrandphotography
Cover Design: © Olaf Glöckler, Atelier Platen, Friedberg

ISBN 978-3-631-77232-4 (Print)
E-ISBN 978-3-631-77787-9 (E-PDF)
E-ISBN 978-3-631-77788-6 (EPUB)
E-ISBN 978-3-631-77789-3 (MOBI)
DOI 10.3726/b15067

© Peter Lang GmbH
Internationaler Verlag der Wissenschaften
Berlin 2018
All rights reserved.

Peter Lang – Berlin · Bern · Bruxelles · New York ·
Oxford · Warszawa · Wien

This publication has been peer reviewed.

www.peterlang.com

Preface

The contributors to this book provide a genuinely scholarly basis for understanding of the philosophical issues on epistemology, ethics and political philosophy. Each author in this book, in relation to their expertise, deals with a problem that has crucial importance in our lives. Every paper in this book should be accessible to non-philosophers as well as philosophers and should engage non-academics as well as academics. Any preface provides an opportunity to thank those who have contributed in the production of a work. Therefore, we would like to express our sincere thanks to the contributors for sharing their expertise.

Eray Yağanak
Ahmet Umut Hacifevzioğlu
Editors

Contents

Notes on Contributors

Ahmet Umut Hacıfevzioğlu is an Assistant Professor in the Department of Sociology at Nişantaşı University in İstanbul, Turkey. He has published articles on Marsilius of Padua, Machiavelli, Montesquieu and Hannah Arendt in English and in Turkish. His research has focused on the statesman, power, and freedom. His areas of interest are political philosophy and ethics.

Aret Karademir is an Assistant professor in the Department of Philosophy at Middle East Technical University. He received his PhD in philosophy from University of South Florida. His areas of research are social and political philosophy, existentialism, and queer theory. Dr. Karademir is the author of *Queering Multiculturalism: Liberal Theory, Ethnic Pluralism, and the Problem of Minorities-within-Minorities*. He has also published several articles on Foucault, Butler, Heidegger, and National Socialism.

Elif Çırakman is an Associate Professor in the Department of Philosophy at Middle East Technical University in Ankara, Turkey. She has published articles on Kant, Hegel, William James, Heidegger and Levinas in English and in Turkish. Her research has focused on the subjects of time, imagination, memory, freedom, desire, and more recently on the ideas of life and hope. Her areas of interest are metaphysics, German idealism, American pragmatism, phenomenology, existentialism and philosophy of life.

Emrah Konuralp is an Assistant Professor in the Department of Political Science and International Relations at İstanbul Yeni Yüzyıl University in İstanbul, Turkey. He earned his BS, MS and PhD degrees from the Department of Political Science and Public Administration at Middle East Technical University in Ankara, Turkey. He has published articles on identity, multiculturalism, nationalism, postsecularism, theories of state. His areas of interest are gender politics, identity, theories of nationalism and ethnicity, secularisation, comparative politics, Turkish politics. He is the Editor-in-Chief of biannually published refereed journal on social sciences, *Lectio Socialis*.

Eray Yağanak is an Assistant Professor in the Department of Philosophy at Mersin University in Mersin, Turkey. His areas of research are ethics, social and political philosophy. He received his PhD in philosophy from Middle East Technical University. He has published several articles on ethics, human rights, human nature, violence, identity and politics. He is the editor of *Philosophical*

Conversations and *Identity Politics and Minority Problem* published in Turkish. He is the Editor-in-Chief of biannually published journal of *Kilikya Felsefe Dergisi* and President of the *Association of the Social and Political Philosophy* (Toplum ve Siyaset Felsefesi Derneği) established in Turkey.

Fulden İbrahimhakkıoğlu is an Assistant Professor of Philosophy at Middle East Technical University, where she teaches courses on social and political philosophy, ethics, feminist philosophy, and queer philosophy. She has published journal articles and book chapters on war, masculinity, and the nation-state, transnational feminism, decolonial philosophy, philosophy of the body and affect, as well as on the intellectual heritage of some modern and contemporary Continental thinkers, including Descartes, Nietzsche, and Foucault. Broadly speaking, her research revolves around the question of the body and its political bearings from a decolonial feminist perspective.

İsmail Serin is a faculty member at the Department of Philosophy, Ondokuz Mayıs University in Samsun. He received his PhD in Kant's philosophy. He is currently working on Adorno's critique of Husserl's epistemology.

Mehmet Şiray is a lecturer in Philosophy Department at Mimar Sinan Fine Arts University in İstanbul, Turkey. He received his PhD in philosophy from Johannes Gutenberg University of Mainz. He has published various articles on G. Bataille, B. Spinoza, R. Girard, J. Rancière and J. L. Nancy related to philosophy of art, aesthetics, contemporary philosophy and literary theory. He is the author of *Performance and Performativity* published by Peter Lang in 2009.

Ahmet Umut Hacıfevzioğlu

Critique of Liberal Parliamentary Democracy in the Context of Carl Schmitt

In *The Concept of Political,* Schmitt conceptualized his method as examining: "the questions re-suggested each time by new and complicated situations without missing the phenomena within their criteria" (Schmitt, 2014b: 47). He also criticizes rationalism, the dominant paradigm of the Enlightenment. Schmitt presents Marquis de Condorcet as the typical enlightened radical who claims that each concrete thing is the implication of a single general law, and that it is inevitable to transform the absolute rationalism into a dictatorship of the intellect. Instead of comprehending phenomena in their reality, Concordet tried to dictate outside law and identify the law and reality. On the other hand, the dominant paradigm of the Enlightenment was not limited to absolute rationalism. According to the scholars who defend relative rationalism against absolute rationalism, reality appears with public debate in the parliament (Schmitt, 2014a: 71–72). In addition to rationalism, Schmitt claims that technique is one of the phenomena that should be questioned in the context of Enlightenment political relationships.

Schmitt called his era the century of a religious belief in technique and claimed that the soul is hopeless against technique. Other scholars of the era, primarily Heidegger, held the similar views. Schmitt criticizes technique because it is a politically unbiased area. According to him, since the sixteenth century, the European spirit tried to establish several unbiased areas as "central areas" for the resolution of political problems (Esgün, 2013: 497). These central areas were theology in the sixteenth century, metaphysics in the seventeenth century, humanist ethics in the eighteenth century, economics in the nineteenth century and technique in the twentieth century. Although Schmitt says that there is a dominant unbiased area in each era, he does not argue that they are exclusive to each era. For instance, economics and technique also have importance when the theology is at the center, but theology shapes the ideology and activity of the era. Schmitt claims that there are leading elites of the center areas in each era. The clergy was the leading elite of the era when theology was dominant. The economists were the nineteenth century leading elites. So to speak, economists were the clergy of the nineteenth century. Engineers are the elites of the technical age. Ultimately, each era creates its own categories, value systems and elites, and the

Enlightenment and the sixteenth century are different in terms of their categories and values. In each era, problems are intended to be resolved in the context of the unbiased area that is dominant. For instance, in the nineteenth century, problems were to be solved in the context of economics. Schmitt claimed that the transformation from the old to the new meant that the older understanding was neutralized by the new one (Kardeş, 2015: 37). This neutralization also includes the theory of the state. Schmitt's theories of the state and democracy can be clarified by the meaning he imposed on the concept of the political.

Of leftist Heideggerian scholars, Schmitt was the first to introduce the difference between politics and the political which is deeply affecting today's political philosophy. Political philosophers prior to Schmitt usually considered politics on its own and did not ask what makes other areas political. However, Schmitt's distinction between politics and the political is similar to the Heiddegerian distinction between *existence* and *existing* as described by Marchart, who claims that politics is an ontic platform that includes discourses and institutions to provide order and imply the categories of the political, antagonism and specificity (cited by Esgün, 2013: 504). According to Schmitt, the concept of politics has a specific category just as ethics, aesthetics and economics have specific categories. Schmitt defined categories as good and bad in morals, beautiful and ugly in the aesthetics, and useful or harmful in economics. He claimed that the specific political category that can be used to explain political activities and motives is the distinction between friend and enemy. The category of friend-enemy cannot explain the content of the concept of the political, but functions as a conceptual form. The function of the friend and enemy category explains the degree of integration or discrimination. Taking into account Schmitt's concept of the political, any religious, moral, economic, ethnic or other opposition only becomes a political opposition by effectively dividing people into friends or enemies (Schmitt, 2014b: 67). In other words, the concept of the political concerns the distinction between enemy and friend, rather than enmity alone, and assumes both enemy and friend as prior (Schmitt, 2017: 119). In the context of Schmitt's concept of the political, Marxism and liberalism struggled to substitute politics with economic categories and were on the same side. However, Schmitt claims that politics is practically and theoretically independent from all economic, moral, aesthetic or other categories. Schmitt believes that political enmity can have many different origins. The political differs from other spheres of value in that it is not based on a substantive distinction of its own. The ethical, for example, is based on a distinction between the morally good and the morally bad, the aesthetic on a distinction between the beautiful and the ugly, and economics is based on a distinction between the profitable and the unprofitable.

"The objectivity and autonomy of the concept of the political is confirmed by its resting upon an indigenous distinction, as it were–that of friend and enemy" (Schmitt, 2014b: 57–58). In Schmitt's political understanding, the enemy is not reducible to a rival or opponent, but a collective identity and difference based on people. In other words, collectives fight with each other. If this kind of collective is based on the entire public, the enemy is a public enemy and has public characteristics (Schmitt, 2014b: 59). Schmitt defines public freedom in the context of the friend-enemy category, and explains that the freedom of a society is based on the decisions that they can make regarding their enemies. In other words, it is only possible to talk about the freedom of a society if its people are able to decide who their enemies are (Schmitt, 2014b: 79–80). Schmitt points out that a community that does not make the friend-enemy distinction is not free and loses its political characteristics, and he questions the notion of the state of his era in the context of political.

According to Schmitt, all the significant terms of the theory of state in the modern era are forms of secularized theology. God assumes the secular form of an almighty legislature in the modern era (Schmitt. 2005: 36). The legislature's secular form is the state. Liberal theory's concept of the state reduces it to an objective judge, reduces politics to the parliament, and for Schmitt, has lost its political characteristics. Therefore, the notion of the liberal state of the modern era marks a process of de-politicization. However, by arguing that "the concept of the political is preceded by the concept of state" (Schmitt, 2014b: 49), Schmitt points out that all regimes, whether *polis, imperium* or *état*, are open to historical change based on the power of the political, and the existence of state is only possible due to its political features. Taking into account the concept of the political, Schmitt derives no specific political idea from the concept of liberalism. Liberalism only makes it possible to polemicize against the state and its institutions. A polemicist liberal politics is not criticism of the political, but liberal criticism of politics. The liberal theory that focuses on individual struggle against state authority demands the limitation and control of state authority to protect individual freedom and private property, attempting to transform it to a judge. It also develops several methods to balance monarchy and democracy. Liberal ideology slightly involves the state and the political, but mainly features morality and economics instead (Schmitt, 2014b: 100–101). Schmitt says that it is not possible for liberalism, which tries to establish an order based on separation of powers and balance while trying to link the political to morality and subordinate it to economics, to develop a theory of the state or a principle of political foundations (Schmitt, 2014b: 91). In other words, Schmitt classifies political tendencies as having or not having a concept of the political, but not in the context of ideologies, and he claims that while liberal theory tries to substitute the political with the morality and economics, no effort should be made to save an individual's life. Therefore, liberal theory that transforms into all areas of human life into areas of specialization does not allow for the political.

Schmitt claims that there is no modernity other than the struggle with the political, and in it, the political is replaced by organizational, technical and economic tasks. The economic and technical ideology that is dominant in the modern era no longer comprehends the political, and the modern state is transforming into what Max Weber thought it would, a big factory. In this factory, economic, technical and organizational intellect is dominant (Schmitt, 2010: 68), and the political is replaced by economic competition and discussion of the concept of morality. In the view of liberal theory, the public that is politically united has an interest in culture, is employed by organizations and is a consumer group (Schmitt, 2014b: 102). Schmitt says that this marks a political crisis. Schmitt notes that the tradition of liberal ideology is mainly responsible for the political crisis that emerged in the twentieth century with the end of the state, and his criticisms on this ideology also means the criticisms of political philosophy affected by Romanticism and Enlightenment philosophy. Schmitt says that although romanticism and rationalism are viewed as opposites, they complete each other because they constitute the main patterns of liberalism in the last instance. Examining the metaphysical origins of liberalism, Schmitt criticizes romanticism's aestheticization of everything, particularly God and the sovereign. Schmitt says that the idea that the state should be objective can be also observed in the understanding of the occasionalist romantic state, which involves a kind of pacifism because it always makes romantic decisions. This reveals the apolitical nature of romanticism (Esgün, 2013: 498–499). In other words, the essence of the liberal perspective is a specific relation to reality that is always transformed into a competitive function. Liberal theory avoids absolute judgment about reality. In this context, freedom of thought, freedom of the press, freedom of assembly and freedom of debate are useful and practical for liberalism as well as existentially important. Negotiation and openness, the trademarks of liberalism, are only possible with freedom of the press (Schmitt, 2014a: 56–57). The liberal bourgeoisie only demands negotiation and openness and defends the freedom of press to achieve them, but it actually requires a proper state for its interests. Schmitt says that the liberal bourgeoisie wants a God, but this God should be neutral. It wants a monarch, but this monarch should not have power. The liberal bourgeoisie's desire for freedom and equality is to guarantee the effect of education and ownership on legislative. Schmitt says that the liberal bourgeoisie removes ancestral aristocracy, but allows the hegemony of the worst type of the aristocracy, the money aristocracy. It accepts neither the hegemony of the king nor of the public (Schmitt, 2010: 63). The concepts of freedom and supremacy of law are included in the focus of liberal state's constitution, which is shaped by the expectations of liberal bourgeoisie.

Schmitt claims that the ideology of bourgeois freedom relies on two principles, division of powers and governance. According to liberal theory, while the state should be limited and divided, individual freedom should be extended and unlimited. For this reason, the principle of division of powers is included in the fundamentals of the state of law. The ability of legislative, executive and judicial branches to limit each other's power is compatible with the bourgeoisie's ideal of a limited state. Schmitt points out that every state is a state of law because they establish certain orders of norms, but that the bourgeoisie state of law relies on the dominance of its own law (cited by Kardeş, 2015: 156). However, the supremacy of law actually means legalizing a certain status quo, which the classes whose political powers and economic interests are stabilized by the law seek to maintain (Schmitt, 2014b: 97). In the end, the principle of the supremacy of law that is defended by liberal theory actually reflects a socially unified demand to serve bourgeois interests and norms, but defending the supremacy of norms means seeing the state as a servant that enables liberal theory's freedoms instead of seeing the political structure as a constituent power. In other words, norms make the state a servant that makes freedoms possible. Given Schmitt's concept of the political, constitutional and public law loses its political function in a state where the supremacy of norms is dominant.

However, according to Schmitt, there is no norm that is applicable to chaos. Norms cannot act on their own, so it is impossible for them to function in situations with no order or in a state of emergency. Schmitt says that the exception is more interesting than the normal situation, since the ordinary sovereign norms do not provide any clue about who is sovereign (Schmitt, 2010: 22). In other words, Schmitt objects to the rationalist scheme in which everything is under the control of the human mind and ideals shape realities, and he moves the focus of political ideology from epistemology to ontology. The exception emerges as a contingent phenomenon that re-establishes the fundamentals every time (Esgün, 2013: 503). For this reason, Schmitt questions the relationship between the concept of sovereign and norms. Schmitt says that: "the sovereign is the one that decides the state of emergency" (Schmitt, 2005: 5). Schmitt thinks sovereignty is a borderline concept based on the exception because sovereignty, unlike the constitutional function of the state of law, is present in extraordinary situations without being subjected to supervision. Since the rationalist scheme is blind to what should be done in the state of emergency, neither being right nor being wise is required to produce law, despite the claims of legal discourse (Esgün, 2013: 501). As Hobbes said: "covenants, without the sword, are but words and of no strength to secure a man at all" (Hobbes, 2014: 227). Schmitt says that authority makes law, not truth. Therefore, Schmitt's state of emergency refers to a general theory of the state, not to a decree of a state of emergency. The decision on the state of emergency is a decision in the full sense of the word, since a general norm that never includes an absolute exception does not provide a basis for what should be done in a state of emergency (Schmitt, 2005: 5). When a state of law ceases to function in the state of emergency, the constitution is only able to determine who is authorized to intervene, and the decision also shows who is sovereign. In other words, the sovereign decides whether there is a state of emergency and what to do about it. The sovereign is authorized to suspend the constitution entirely and operate outside the ordinary legal order (Schmitt, 2005: 6–7). Therefore, Schmitt requires a strong state that can make absolute decisions and end chaos like the Roman Catholic Church. In each crisis, a *katechon*[*] emerges to notice the situation, warn and supervise people by informing them about judgment day. This *katechon* in Christian eschatology is the opposite of chaos and represents the sovereign in politics. None of the norms can guide during chaos, so the sovereign suspends the law to realize the norm, end antagonisms and reestablish political order and stability (Esgün, 2013: 502–503). Therefore, the essence of sovereignty lies in the decision. Schmitt defines the sovereign as a decision-making monopoly rather than a legal force or monopoly on governing (Schmitt, 2010: 20–21). The decision is an autonomous value independent from definitive justification. It emerges from nothing from the normative perspective. The legal power of the decision is different than the outcome of justification. Decisions are not made by means of a norm, instead a decision determines what is a norm (Schmitt, 2010: 37). In the end, Schmitt says that the meaning of the state of emergency for the law is similar to the meaning of a miracle for theology. The view of modern state of law has been conquered by deism and theology excludes miracles from the world and metaphysics. This theology and metaphysics rejects the violation of natural law both as exception and as divine intervention, but Schmitt sees the state of emergency as having the nature of a miracle instantiated in the direct intervention of the sovereign in the legal order.

---

[*] *Katechon* is a Greek word meaning "that which withholds" or "one that withholds." It is a biblical concept found in the writing of St. Paul in his letter to the Thessalonians. It has become a major point of focus in political. While the term as used by St. Paul has soteriological implications within the context of the story of salvation in Christianity, the term has become a "secularized" concept of the political.

Enlightenment rationalism rejects all types of state of emergency (Schmitt, 2010: 41–42) while it keeps some distance from the traditional definition in the context of the notion of legitimacy.

In the past, all theist and excessive approaches executed in the context of legitimacy on the state theory, were replaced by a new legitimacy notion. In other words, while the notion of traditional legitimacy is replaced by the notion of democratic legitimacy based on the society's constituent power where the theory of public law is positivized (Schmitt. 2010: 54), the ideology regarding that the Europe should democratize had been widely accepted among the French intellectuals since 1830s. Alexis de Tocqueville is one of these intellectuals (Schmitt, 2000: 23). The introduction to Tocqueville's *Democracy in America* argues that in time democracy will irresistibly and universally dominate the entire world, and there will be gradual progress in equality together with democracy (Tocqueville, 2015: 31). Tocqueville claims that the state that emerges from the alliance of democracy and parliamentarianism is a politically objective mediator that negotiates conflicting interests through law with no discrimination (Esgül, 2013: 498). However, Schmitt's view is that democracy is not based on difference or minority, but on identity.

Schmitt defines democracy as an identification problem, and democracy is considered identical with the republic by the bourgeoisie, which is a political regime usually based on the domination of the majority and sometimes on the domination of the minority. On the other hand, as the essence of democracy, all decisions made are valid for all citizens. Therefore, in democracies, it is assumed that the will of the minority is usually identical with the will of majority, reflecting Rousseau's *general will*. The notion of *general will* introduced in Rousseau's *The Social Contract* is a basis for democratic thinking. According to Rousseau, sovereignty cannot be transferred to others and also cannot be represented. Sovereignty is based on the *general will*, which cannot be represented. Therefore, all laws that are not approved by the society are invalid (Rousseau, 2006: 90). According to John Locke, who prioritized Rousseau's legal thought, each citizen leaves his own natural sovereignty to continuous rules constituted by the community of citizens for their objective and impartial protection (Locke, 2016: 94). Locke and Rousseau's arguments are based on the traditional democratic view that citizens have to agree with laws that conflict with their individual will, since the law is the will of free citizens. Both thinkers associate law and the *general will* of the citizens. On the other hand, Schmitt says: "Thus a citizen never really gives his consent to a specific content but rather in abstract to the result that evolves out of the *general will*, and he votes only so that the votes out of which one can know this *general will* can be calculated. If the result deviates from the intention of those individuals voting, then the outvoted know that they have mistaken the content of the *general will*." One can justify the rule of the minority over the majority, even while appealing to democracy. Therefore, the argument that claims law and public will are identical as the essence of the democratic principle. In other words, it really makes no difference whether one identifies the will of the majority or the will of the minority with the will of the people because it can never be the absolutely unanimous will of all citizens (Schmitt, 2014a: 41–42). On the other hand, the individualist arguments of defenders of liberal democracy imply the end of the political. In other words, when the voting system reduces individuals to the status of voters, it removes the possibility of the political because the decision-making process by voting is not a real political decision. Schmitt sees the proposal that the majority decides as a mystification of modern politics rather than a constitutional problem. Society is the subject of the constituent power, which is outside all norms connected to constitutional acts. Therefore, as a political entity, the public cannot be defined by norms. All democracies require the existence of public opinion. The powers of government candidates are chosen by the citizens. However, Schmitt claims that the parliamentary system and parties tend to divide the public as the most basic characteristic of democracy. Accordingly, parties rely on identity as a democratic argument and violate the principle of representation. Schmitt thinks that liberal organizations and functions conflict with democracy as a political style, and the citizen belongs in the political arena in democracy. This means that defining the citizen as a political statement is only possible through his public presence. Therefore, the citizen is not an individual, but the subject of a *polis*. However, merchants are entrepreneurs. For this reason, it is not possible for a bourgeois individual to be an element of democracy. The argument of the principle of equality of the liberal understanding does not intend to make the political existence of the bourgeoisie possible, but to support and maintain its economic existence and freedom to own property. Schmitt criticizes the liberal understanding by revealing the public and non-bourgeois character of the democracy, and claims that as an apolitical principle, democracy is not a liberal notion. The thinker says that only the public's *potestas* makes democracy possible as a political principle. In other words, a democratic process is based on the public will. However, since liberal constitutional theory advocates constitutional democracy rather than public-based democracy, it conflicts with the notion of democracy based on public will. In a democracy, the public will should not be defined by the constitution, but the constitution should define public will. While the bourgeoisie's perception of the principle of the supremacy of the law removes the possibility of politics, it also reduces democracy to merely elections and referendums (Kardeş, 2015: 163–167). Schmitt claimed that the alliance of liberalism with democracy is temporary and contingent, and while liberal democrats struggle to give it a legal and pluralist character, they define democracy with content that suits their own preferences (Gottfried, 1990: 4). This notion is indispensable to the instrumentalization of democracy. However, the political movement that struggles to instrumentalize democracy for its own purposes is not limited to liberalism.

Schmitt claims that socialism emerged as a new ideology in the nineteenth century and prefers to form alliances with democracies. While the socialist organization of the German working class expressed progressive democratic discourses, it almost became a pioneer of radical ideologies beyond the bourgeoisie democracy. The working class undertook the double task of meeting both socialist and democratic demands (Schmitt, 2014a: 38–39), but to the extent that it was realized, democracy served many masters and had no substantial, clear goal. Social democracy joined with socialism in the nineteenth century, and the success of Napoleon III and the results of Swiss referenda demonstrate that it could actually be conservative and reactionary, just as Proudhon foresaw. If all political tendencies could make use of democracy, then this proved that it had no political content and was only an organizational form (Schmitt, 2014a: 39–40). Schmitt claims that democracy is only a form without content that can thus be used by different political tendencies. The various nations or social and economic groups who organize themselves democratically have the same subject, the people, only in the abstract. However, concretely, the masses are sociologically and psychologically heterogeneous. A democracy can be militarist or pacifist, absolutist or liberal, centralized or decentralized, progressive or reactionary (Schmitt, 2014a: 41). Schmitt refers to Proudhon's ideas about how democracy functions as a form in the context of the alliance between liberalism and democracy. As Proudhon claimed in *The Principles of Federation*, the forms of the liberal or democratic state correspond to the generative principle and developmental law of this system. In a liberal or democratic state, the distribution of the governmental roles among the citizens makes them public officials, a new social class. Proudhon says that from that moment, democracy is in danger because the state separates itself from the nation, and this new class of citizens, its personnel, practically become what they were under the monarchy, more loyal to the prince than to the state (Proudhon, 2014: 36–37). On the other hand, in liberal democracies, the notions of both individuals and groups regarding the objectivity of the state cause competition among interest groups, leading to the capture of the state by political parties in parliamentary politics (Dyzenhaus, 1999: 38). Such a democracy raises the question of how the state officials can observe Aristotle's *common good* of the citizens. Therefore, Schmitt asserted the need to question the identity between the governor and the governed, the subject and the object of state authority, in the context of representing the commoners in parliament and law (Schmitt, 2014a: 42). According to Schmitt, the identities assumed by democratic arguments are possible only in the formal context. However, the concrete phenomena indicate that these identities cannot be established. For instance, the masses can be persuaded by the propaganda and manipulation (Schmitt, 2014a: 43). It is debatable if a will that emerges in such an environment can reflect the public will. A will that emerges in a manipulated environment is not public, but actually the will of the manipulators. In that case, the main problem is who dominates the tools that are used to shape the public will. Militaries, political powers and party organs can govern these tools (Schmitt, 2014a: 45). Therefore, the power that should be led by the public will actually shapes the public will.

Another issue that can be questioned in the context of democracy is related to its destiny. Since it can serve so many masters, democracy can serve political movements that desire to destroy it by using it as a tool. This is the tragedy of democracy: giving up democracy in the name of defending democracy at all costs or giving up democracy for the sake of being a democrat. Since the possibility of being democrat at any price in democracies is open to the discussion (Schmitt, 2014a: 44), the argument that the parliament is indispensable to democracy can also be falsified. Schmitt suggested that if democracy is possible without a modern parliament, a parliament without democracy is also possible (Schmitt, 2014a: 49). In the parliament, government emerges from the parliament. In other words, the executive is under the sway of the legislative, but for practical reasons it is impossible today for everyone to gather at the same time in one place, so, quite reasonably, a committee of responsible people is elected, and parliament is precisely that. The familiar formula is that parliament is a committee of the people, and the government is a committee of parliament. If for practical and technical reasons the representatives of the people can decide instead of the people themselves, then certainly a single trusted representative could also decide in the name of the same people without ceasing to be democratic, and the argument would justify an anti-parliamentary Caesarism (Schmitt, 2014a: 51–52). On the other hand, the *ratio* of parliament rests on a dynamic dialectic based on the confrontation between differences of opinion, from which the real political will results. In other words, the main function of the parliament is public negotiation (Schmitt, 2014a: 53), although it is known all along that the will determined in the context of negotiated decisions is the will of political group with the majority in the parliament. The government constituted by the representatives of the political group with the majority in the parliament implements the will of the majority in the parliament. Therefore, the practical implementation of Locke and Montesquieu's arguments about balancing legislative and executive powers is questionable. Although the principle of the division of powers was suggested by John Locke, Montesquieu was the first thinker to describe their roles clearly. According to Montesquieu, there are three powers in a state where the constitution is based on freedom: legislative, executive and judicial. "In every government there are three sorts of power: the legislative; the executive, in respect to things dependent on the law of nations; and the executive, in regard to matters that depend on the civil law" (Montesquieu, 2017: XI. 6, 198). The holders of these three powers should be restrained by and represent different actors such as the monarch, nobles and the commoners, which makes it possible to protect liberties. When the legislative and executive powers are united in the same person or in the same body of magistrates, there can be no liberty: "because apprehensions may arise, lest the same monarch or senate should enact tyrannical laws, to execute them in a tyrannical manner" (Montesquieu, 2017: XI. 6, 199). However, problems with the practical implementation of the principle of division of powers show that there is no strong distinction between the powers that Locke and Montesquieu tried to delineate. Therefore, the identification of the public will with democracy in the context of democratic arguments is falsifiable.

Conclusion

The parliamentary criticisms of Carl Schmitt occur primarily in the context of his concept of the political. The liberal parliamentary democracy that addresses the state and society with economic and ethical motives intends to destroy the friend-enemy distinction that makes the political possible. According to Schmitt, the liberal parliamentary democracy that features economic competition and negotiation instead of the friend-enemy distinction is an attempt to build a state that suits the purposes of the profit-seeking bourgeoisie. For this reason, he sees liberal parliamentary democracy as a political movement used as a tool by the state for its economic interests. The state, the greatest outcome of modernity in Schmitt's view, should not serve the interests of a certain class (for Marx) and should have autonomous power. However, protecting the interests of the bourgeoisie both with the emphasis on individualism and discourses on the state of law discourse means hollowing out the content of democracy. Schmitt's view of liberalism and parliamentary democracy as a governance style make it possible to discern the protection of hierarchies in society instead of the establishment of social identity. Schmitt claims that liberal parliamentary democracy can only protect these hierarchies by comprehending democracy as the identity of the governor and the governing.

References

Dyzenhaus, D. (1999). *Legality and Legitimacy: Carl Schmitt, Hans Kelsen and Hermann Heller in Weimar*, Oxford: Oxford University Press.

Esgün, G. T. (2013). "Carl Schmitt", Ahu Tunçel ve Kurtul Gülenç (Ed). *Siyaset Felsefesi Tarihi* içinde (s. 495–511). Ankara: Doğu Batı Yayınları.

Gottfried, P. E. (1990). *Carl Schmitt: Politics and Theory*, New York: Greenwood Press.

Hobbes, T. (2014). "Leviathan", *Batı'da Siyasal Düşünceler Tarihi*, 5. Baskı, (Çev.) Lim, S., (Der.), Tunçay, M., İstanbul: İstanbul Bilgi Üniversitesi Yayınları.

Kardeş, M. E. (2015). *Schmitt'le Birlikte Schmitt'e Karşı*, İstanbul: İletişim.

Locke, J. (2016). *Yönetim Üzerine İkinci İnceleme*, (Çev.) Bakırcı, F., Ankara: Eksi Kitaplar.

Montesquieu. (2017). *Kanunların Ruhu Üzerine*. (Çev) Günen, B., İstanbul: Türkiye İş Bankası Kültür Yayınları.

Proudhon, J. P. (2014). *Federasyon İlkesi*, (Çev.) Özsalan, M., İstanbul: Öteki Yayınevi.

Rousseau, J. J. (2006). *Toplum Sözleşmesi*, (Çev.) Günyol, V., İstanbul: Türkiye İş Bankası Kültür Yayınları.

Schmitt, C. (2000). *The Crisis of Parliamentary Democracy*, (Trans.) Kennedy, E., Cambridge, Massachusetts, and London, England: The MIT Press.

Schmitt, C. (2014a). *Parlamenter Demokrasinin Krizi*, (Çev.) Zeybekoğlu, A. E., Ankara: Dost Kitabevi Yayınları.

Schmitt, C. (2005). *Political Theology*, (Trans.) Schwab G., Chicago: University of Chicago Press.

Schmitt, C. (2010). *Siyasal İlahiyat*, (Çev.) Zeybekoğlu, A. E., Ankara: Dost Kitabevi Yayınları.

Schmitt, C. (2014b). *Siyasal Kavramı*, (Çev.) Göztepe. E., İstanbul: Metis Yayınları.

Schmitt, C. (2017). *Partizan Teorisi*, (Çev.) Bekiroğlu. S., Ankara: Nika Yayınevi.

Tocqueville, A. (2015). *Amerika'da Demokrasi*, (Çev.) Doğan. Ö, Ankara: Doğu Batı Yayınları.

Aret Karademir

Heidegger as a Modern Spiritualist: A Foucauldian Interpretation

Introduction

In his 1981–1982 *Collège de France* lecture-course, *The Hermeneutics of the Subject*, Michel Foucault makes a distinction between philosophy and what he calls "spirituality." By philosophy he understands "the form of thought that asks [...] what determines that there is and can be truth and falsehood and whether or not we can separate the true and the false," as well as the form of inquiry that questions "what it is that enables the subject to have access to the truth" and "attempts to determine the conditions and limits of the subject's access to the truth" (Foucault, 2005: 15). By spirituality, on the other hand, he refers to "the search, practice, and experience through which the subject carries out the necessary transformations on himself in order to have access to the truth" (Foucault, 2005: 15). In other words, spirituality refers to the set of techniques and exercises, what we may call "spiritual exercises," such as "purifications, ascetic exercises, [and] renunciations," as well as "meditation, meditation on death, meditation on future evils, [and] the examination of conscience," whose aim is to transform the subject in its being, so that it becomes capable of having access to the truth (Foucault, 2005: 15, 417).

Foucault claims that according to the tradition of spirituality, which unfolded itself from the 5th century AD to the 5th century BC, including Ancient Greek, Hellenistic, Roman, and Early Christian traditions of thought, the subject cannot have access to the truth unless it exposes itself to a certain self-transformation. Thus, in those ancient traditions of thought, "the philosophical question of 'how to access to the truth' and the practice of spirituality (of the necessary transformations in the very being of the subject which will allow access to the truth) [...] were never separate" (Foucault, 2005: 17). In short, for Foucault, Greek, Hellenistic, Roman, and Early Christian traditions of thought were characterized by the *epimeleia heautou*; that is, by "the care of the self" and, therefore, by "a number of actions exercised on the self by the self, actions by which one takes responsibility for oneself and by which one changes, purifies, transforms, and transfigures oneself" (Foucault, 2005: 11).

Foucault argues that in the tradition of spirituality, *epimeleia heautou* was always "coupled or twinned with" the principle of *gnôthi seauton* (know yourself), and that there was a circular relation between *epimeleia heautou* and *gnôthi seauton*, such that the subject could not transform itself without knowing the truth of its Self and that the truth of the Self could not be entirely unveiled without the transformation of the subject was completed (Foucault, 2005: 4). As a result, the subject had to know the truth of its Self and at the same time transform this Self in order to have access to the truth. Thus, in Foucault's words, there was "a circular relation between self-knowledge, knowledge of the truth, and care of the self" (Foucault, 2005: 255). However, Foucault claims that the tradition of spirituality became obsolete in the age of modern schools of thought, especially when "the Cartesian approach" placed "self-evidence"—rather than self-transformation—at the core of systematic thinking, and when "formal conditions, objective conditions, formal rules of method, [and] the structure of the object to be known" replaced the principles of *epimeleia heautou* and *gnôthi seauton* in such a way that the subject did not have to expose itself to any transformation *in its being* anymore in order to have access to the truth (Foucault, 2005: 14, 18).

Nevertheless, Foucault suggests that it is possible to read nineteenth century philosophy as an attempt to resuscitate the tradition of spirituality. He states: "Read again all of nineteenth century philosophy—well, almost all: Hegel anyway, Schelling, Schopenhauer, Nietzsche, the Husserl of the *Krisis*, and Heidegger as well—and you see precisely here also that knowledge, the activity of knowing [...] is nonetheless still linked to the requirements of spirituality"; that is, "to a transformation in the subject's being" (Foucault, 2005: 28). The name of Heidegger is especially important for Foucault, because he believes that "only Heidegger and Lacan" systematically problematized the relationship between the subject and the truth in the twentieth century. They asked "What is involved in the case of the subject and of the truth? And: What is the relationship of the subject to the truth. What is the subject of truth, what is the subject who speaks the truth?" (Foucault, 2005: 189). Foucault also states, without explaining himself, that he "tried to reflect on all this from the side of Heidegger and starting from Heidegger" (Foucault, 2005: 189). My aim in this chapter is to "read again" Heidegger's early philosophy, especially his *Being and Time*, from the perspective of the tradition of spirituality. I will argue that we can interpret Heidegger's early philosophy as a form of modern spirituality, and his *existential analytic of Dasein* as a spiritual exercise, which aims at the transformation of the subject/Dasein in order to have access to the truth/Being.

Reading Heidegger from the perspective of Foucault's interpretation of the tradition of spirituality is important for several reasons. Firstly, in his last interview in 1984, Foucault states that "For me Heidegger has always been the essential philosopher [...]. My entire philosophical development was determined by my reading of Heidegger" (Foucault, 1988: 250). However, he did not explain what aspects of Heidegger's philosophy influenced him. Moreover, Foucault rarely refers to Heidegger in his writings. Reading Heidegger from the perspective of Foucault's interpretation of the tradition of spirituality may help us come one step closer to understanding the relationship between Foucault and Heidegger, as well as uncovering the Heideggerian aspects of Foucault's understanding of resistance to power, which may allow us to deliberate on the relation between ethics (self-transformation), epistemology (truth), and politics (resistance). Secondly, as will be clarified below, reading Heidegger's existential analytic of Dasein as a spiritual exercise may help us see how Heidegger's early philosophy and his *Kehre* in the late 1930s are connected. This may give us some insight in interpreting the reasons behind Heidegger's attempt to investigate the thoughts of major figures in the history of Being; that is, in interpreting the reasons behind his insistence on the need for *Seinsgeschichte* for asking the question of Being.

Spirituality in *Being and Time*

Heidegger's aim in *Being and Time* is to ask the question of Being and unveil "the meaning of Being." He argues that the task at hand requires the determination of an entity that must be privileged in any interrogation into the meaning of Being, as well as the disclosure of this entity in its being. Heidegger asks: "In *which* entities is the meaning of Being to be discerned? From which entities is the disclosure of Being to take its departure?" (Heidegger, 1962: 26). It is worth noting that Heidegger uses "the meaning of Being" and "the disclosure of Being" synonymously. The reason is that by "meaning" he understands "that wherein the intelligibility of something maintains itself," i.e., "*the 'upon which' of a projection in terms of which something becomes intelligible as something*" (Heidegger, 1962: 193). Hence, the meaning of an entity is the ground upon which that entity becomes intelligible to human beings and, therefore, becomes an object of meaningful statements with truth value. Similarly, entities need "disclosure" (*aletheia*, unconcealment), so that they are taken "out of their hiddenness" and, thus, become intelligible objects of true or false statements (Heidegger, 1962: 262). In short, just like meaning, *aletheia* refers to the ground wherein the intelligibility of entities maintains itself. It is also worth noting that the term Heidegger uses for "truth" is nothing but *aletheia*. Hence, it is safe to say that Heidegger's aim in *Being and Time* is to have access to *the truth of Being*.

Heidegger argues that the entity whose disclosure in its being is the *sine qua non* for having access to the truth of Being is human beings, namely Dasein. This is because "Dasein is an entity which does not just occur among other entities. Rather it is ontically distinguished by the fact that, in its very Being, that Being is an *issue* for it" (Heidegger, 1962: 32). Moreover, "*Understanding of Being is itself a definite characteristic of Dasein's Being*" (Heidegger, 1962: 32). As a result, knowledge of the Self, or the truth of Dasein, is the *sine qua non* for having access to the truth of Being. That is, as in the tradition of ancient spirituality, the subject/Dasein cannot have access to the truth unless it knows itself in its being. This is the reason why Heidegger begins his investigation into the meaning of Being with the existential analytic of Dasein. Moreover, as will be clarified below, Dasein's self-knowledge requires and is linked with the transformation of its Self. Hence, Dasein cannot know its Self, and, therefore, cannot have access to the truth (of Being), without exposing its Self to a certain transformation.

According to Heidegger's existential analytic, Dasein is not "the egocentric individual," but "Being-in-the-world" (Heidegger, 1962: 65; Heidegger, 1984: 137). The world in question refers to the socio-historically *shared* public world that Dasein was born or "thrown" into. In Heidegger's words "the world is always the one that I share with Others. The world of Dasein is a *with-world* [*Mitwelt*, social world]" (Heidegger, 1962: 155). The socio-historically shared world functions as a context of meaning for Dasein and provides Dasein with the norms and standards of intelligibility. Specifically, the world draws the boundaries of intelligible ways of existence, intelligible patterns of conduct, intelligible modes of interpreting entities, and intelligible forms of self-understanding for human beings. Hence, it determines what it means *to be*—for example, to be a successful professor, to be a decent behavior, or to be a meaningful statement. Thus, in each socio-historically shared world prevails an "understanding of Being," i.e., "that which determines entities as entities, that on the basis of which entities are already understood" (Heidegger, 1962: 25–26).

Heidegger argues that Dasein acquires its identity by "projecting" itself upon "possible ways for it to be," ones that are provided to Dasein by the historical world it was *contingently* born into (Heidegger, 1962: 67). Specifically, Dasein becomes what it is by *performing* certain social roles in certain, socio-historically possible ways and by appropriating certain social norms and standards in taking its life-course into a socio-historically viable direction, as well as by interpreting its Self in socio-historically intelligible ways and by acting accordingly. Dasein's performances, self-interpretations, and stances in life *add up* to making Dasein what it is. Hence, Dasein is "Being-towards-death" (Heidegger, 1962: 294)— not in the sense of being toward the end of its physical life, but in the sense of being "toward self-completion," i.e., toward the "final configuration" of its identity as the end product of its performances and self-interpretations (Guignon,

1983: 134; Guignon, 1985: 332). As Heidegger states in his 1928 lecture-course, *The Metaphysical Foundations of Logic*, Being-towards-death amounts to "being towards oneself" (Heidegger, 1984: 189). This means that Dasein is never complete. It is always on the way to completion, "in its process of realization" (Heidegger, 1984: 139). As a result, Dasein's identity is *historically contingent* and *performative*, in the sense that Dasein is the *incomplete* product of its meaningful *performances* and self-interpretations, whose intelligibility is *contingent upon* the historical world Dasein was *accidentally* thrown into.

Moreover, Dasein is guilty (*schuldig*), because it owes (*verschuldet*) its identity to the norms, standards, and social roles *that are not of its own making*, but the products of the historical world it was *accidentally* thrown into. In this respect, Dasein is, *always already*, self-alienated. In Heidegger's words, "so far as any Dasein factically exists, it *is* also guilty" (Heidegger, 1962: 326). Hence, Dasein is never self-identical and never the absolute basis of its Self, even though its identity depends on *its own* performances, life-choices, and self-interpretations. Dasein has to *take over* its always self-alienated, historically contingent, and incomplete existence, and put it on the way to completion by performing historically contingent social possibilities in historically contingent ways (Heidegger, 1962: 330). As a result, Dasein's Self is not constituted by a self-identical, ahistorical, and already-established essence. Instead, it is performative, contingent, and full of guilt.

Heidegger suggests that in its everyday life, Dasein lacks self-knowledge. It is blind to the truth of its Self—namely to its performativity, contingency, and existential culpability—because of the way in which it exists. Specifically, since Dasein becomes what it is by performing historically possible and socially intelligible roles of the *public world* it was thrown into, Dasein has the tendency to lose itself in *public anonymity* to the point of being deprived of its particularity and individuality. Thus, in its everyday life, Dasein does not problematize what One (*das Man*, the they) does in the public world. Instead, it takes the norms, standards, and social roles of the public world for granted, as if they were natural and inevitable, as if they demanded universal and almost automatic obedience, and as if they could relieve Dasein of its non-delegable task of creating an identity for itself by performing social possibilities without having at its disposal any universal or natural justification for its performances. That is, everyday Dasein blindly embraces the norms, standards, interpretations, and social roles that "the 'they' itself prescribes," and forms the supposition that "one is leading and sustaining a full and genuine 'life'" (Heidegger, 1962: 167, 222). In short, in its everyday life in the shared world of meanings, Dasein is "inauthentic," in the sense that it loses its individuality and particularity in public anonymity and, therefore, becomes alienated from its own/true (*eigen*, authentic) Self. Heidegger writes:

> This Being-with-one-another dissolves one's own Dasein completely into the kind of Being of 'the Others', in such a way, indeed, that the Others, as distinguishable and explicit, vanish more and more. In this inconspicuousness and unascertainability, the real dictatorship of the "they" is unfolded. We take pleasure and enjoy ourselves as *they* [*man*] take pleasure; we read, see, and judge about literature and art as *they* see and judge; likewise we shrink back from the 'great mass' as *they* shrink back; we find 'shocking' what *they* find shocking (Heidegger, 1962: 164).

As a result, inauthentic Dasein, because of its mode of existence in its everyday life, is blind to the truth of its Self, *which is the sine qua non for having access to the truth of Being*. Inauthentic Dasein does not realize that it is Being-in-the-world, in the sense that its identity does not refer to the unconcealment of a natural essence that would relieve Dasein of creating an identity for itself on its own, but is contingent upon the historical world it was accidentally thrown into. It also does not realize that it is Being-towards-death, in the sense that it has to take over its contingent existence in order to create and complete its Self without having any universal or natural justification for its identity-building performances. Lastly, it does not realize that it is guilty, in the sense that whatever identity it creates for itself, this identity will always be contingent upon the norms, standards, interpretations, and social roles that are not of its own making. Heidegger writes: inauthentic Dasein "covers up its ownmost Being-towards-death," its "authentic potentiality for Being its Self," i.e., its performative identity as a historically situated, ongoing project to be accomplished; as an always self-alienated, unfolding life-story to be completed (Heidegger, 1962: 220, 295). Consequently, inauthentic Dasein, because of its mode of existence and of its lack of self-knowledge, is deprived of the possibility of having access to the truth of Being, considering that the disclosure of Dasein in its being is the *sine qua non* for having access to the truth of Being. Hence, as in the tradition of ancient spirituality, Dasein needs to transform its Self and at the same time know this Self in order to have access to the truth.

The Link between Self-Knowledge and Self-Transformation

Heidegger believes that Dasein needs the truth of its Self in order to transform itself, but *at the same time* it needs to be in the process of transforming this Self in order to have access to the truth of its being. Primarily, Heidegger argues that it is only through anxiety (*Angst*) that Dasein can transform its inauthentic existence and become authentic. This is because in anxiety, Dasein comes face to face with the truth of its Self. In Heidegger's words, in anxiety, Dasein is disclosed to itself "as a naked 'that it is and has to be'," while its "'whence' and 'whither' remain in darkness" (Heidegger, 1962: 173). It is also disclosed "as thrown Being-towards-death," as the one who is surrounded by the "insignificance of what is within-the-world," and "as something that understands, projects itself upon possibilities" (Heidegger, 1962, 231–232, 395). That is to say, anxiety reveals to Dasein that *it is* thrown into a world it did not choose, and that there is no internal reason why it was born into *this* world. Hence, Dasein's "whence" is in darkness. Be that as it may, Dasein *has to* make something or someone out of its historically contingent existence by its own performances, self-interpretations, and life-choices; it is Being-towards-death. However, neither its public world, nor anything in its own Self, such as self-identical substance or ahistorical human essence, will provide Dasein with intrinsically meaningful, natural, or universal guidelines for its performances and identity-constructions. Hence, Dasein's "whither," too, is in darkness. After all, Dasein does not have a natural or self-identical substance; its identity refers to nothing but the end product of its *projections*. Moreover, worldly entities, including the norms, standards, and social roles of Dasein's world, are *insignificant* in themselves; they are historically contingent. They cannot justify, once and for all, Dasein's projections.

Lastly, anxiety reveals to Dasein that it is guilty, in the sense that the intelligibility of Dasein's performances is contingent upon the public world it was accidentally thrown into. Dasein has no choice but take over its self-alienated, historically situated, and partially completed existence to create an identity for itself. In Heidegger's terminology, this means that to be anxious is to listen to the voice of one's "conscience" that says guilty. Heidegger writes: "The appeal [of conscience] calls back by calling-forth: it calls Dasein *forth* to the possibility of taking over, in existing, even that thrown entity which it is; it calls Dasein back to its thrownness so as to understand this thrownness as the null basis which it has to take up into existence (Heidegger, 1962: 333).

As a result, anxiety makes Dasein "transparent" (*durchsichtig*) to itself, to the truth of its Self, namely to its performativity, contingency, and existential culpability (Heidegger, 1962: 187). For Heidegger, such transparency or self-knowledge does not just refer to a piece of *theoretical knowledge*. Instead, it is linked with and functions as a precondition for Dasein's self-transformation; that is, Dasein's transforming itself into being authentic. Specifically, as Heidegger argues in his 1929–1930 lecture-course, *The Fundamental Concepts of Metaphysics*, to be anxiously transparent to one's Self "cannot mean simply to make conscious" of that "which was previously unconscious" (Heidegger, 1995: 61). The reason is that being-anxious, and, thereby, knowing the truth of Dasein, is a "fundamental attunement," "a fundamental manner," a "*fundamental way in which* Dasein is as Dasein" (Heidegger, 1995: 67). It is a way in which Dasein exists: "Attunements are the fundamental ways in which we *find* ourselves *disposed* in such and such a way. Attunements are the '*how*' according to which one is such and such a way" (Heidegger, 1995: 67). Accordingly, Heidegger's aim in describing the nature of anxiety in particular, and Dasein's truth in general, cannot be interpreted as an attempt to depict "subjectively coloured experiences or epiphenomenal manifestations of psychological life" (Heidegger, 1995: 283). Instead, it is to transform *his own* manner of existence and become authentic. It is to transform *his own* Dasein. After all, for Heidegger, Dasein is "*in each case mine*" (Heidegger, 1962: 67).

Heidegger argues that authentic Dasein is the one which "'choose[s]' itself and win[s] itself," rather than "lose itself and never win itself" (Heidegger, 1962: 68). It is the one which "*choose[s] itself on purpose*," rather than blindly embracing what is handed down to it by its unquestioned public world and this world's unproblematized norms, standards, and social roles; that is, rather than being lost "in those possibilities which may accidentally thrust themselves upon one" (Heidegger, 1962: 308; Heidegger, 1982: 170). Thus, authentic Dasein is the one which commits itself to "the choosing to choose a kind of Being-one's-Self" (Heidegger, 1962: 314). That is to say, authentic Dasein does not choose certain social possibilities *only because* they are publicly and unquestionably valued in the public world it was accidentally thrown into. Instead, it *chooses* them because it *chooses* to become a particular sort of Dasein, but without being blind to the truth of its choices, namely their having no ground other than the fact that Dasein makes a historically contingent choice to choose certain social roles from the socio-historically shared pool of roles, norms, and standards. Hence, authentic Dasein chooses to take the responsibility of taking care of its Self without suppressing the truth of this Self. In *Being and Time*, Heidegger calls such *second-order choosing* "resoluteness." However, in his 1930 lecture-course, *The Essence of Human Freedom*, he uses the term "freedom." Thus, for Heidegger, free Dasein is the one which is "capable of *accountability*" and "*self-responsibility*"; it is the one which is "willing to take responsibility" of taking over its historically contingent, always self-alienated, and existentially culpable Self, and put it on the way to completion without losing itself in public anonymity and without suppressing its *anxiety-engendering* truth (Heidegger, 2005: 15, 182, 193). In short, authentic, free, or transformed Dasein is the one which listens to the voice of its conscience, embraces its guilt, and, thereby, understands the truth of its Self as a contingent, performative, and existentially culpable being.

As a result, authentic existence, or the transformation of inauthentic existence into freedom, requires the uncovering of the truth of the Self. However, it is worth noting that the relationship between self-knowledge and self-transformation is not unilateral. That is, just as one needs to know oneself in his or her being in order to transform one's Self, so too one needs to be in the process of self-transformation in order to become capable of understanding the truth of his or her Self. Heidegger writes: "Our understanding of the appeal [of conscience] unveils itself as our *wanting to have a conscience*" and as our "readiness for anxiety" (Heidegger, 1962: 314, 342). This means that inauthentic Dasein, which is not ready for anxiety due to its comforting publicness and anonymity, cannot hear correctly the voice of its conscience and, therefore, cannot have access to the truth of its Self. In Heidegger's words, "Losing itself in the publicness and the idle talk of the 'they', it [i.e., inauthentic Dasein] *fails to hear* its own Self in listening to the they-self" (Heidegger, 1962: 315). In short, "in any failure to hear the call or any incorrect hearing of *oneself*, there lies a *definite kind* of Dasein's Being" (Heidegger, 1962: 324). Hence, one cannot hear the call of conscience correctly, unless one is on the way to one's "*ownmost* authentic potentiality for becoming guilty" and "*becoming free* for the call" (Heidegger, 1962: 333–334). Thus, just as freedom or authenticity requires the knowledge of the Self, which is the *sine qua non* for having access to the truth of Being, so too self-knowledge requires freedom and authenticity.

Consequently, as in the tradition of ancient spirituality, for Heidegger, too, there is a circular relation between *epimeleia heautou* and *gnôthi seauton*; between self-knowledge, knowledge of the truth, and self-transformation. In this respect, it would be wrong to group Heidegger's existential analytic of Dasein with any other existential or phenomenological research into the nature of human existence. Heidegger's existential analytic is an attempt to transform one's own Dasein, as much as it is an attempt to know one's Self and have access to the truth of Being. This is the reason why the Heidegger of *Being and Time* can be interpreted as a modern spiritualist, and his existential analytic of Dasein as a spiritual exercise, whose aim is at once self-transformation, self-knowledge, and the disclosure of Being.

Authentic Repetitions as Spiritual Exercises

From this perspective, we can read what Heidegger calls *authentic repetition* as a spiritual exercise, as well. Firstly, Heidegger believes that authentic or not, Dasein is a *historically-situated* entity and, therefore, cannot construct an identity for itself *ex nihilo*. Instead, it has to cite or repeat the *traditional possibilities* of existence of the public world in order to become what it is; that is, in *anticipating* the final configuration of its identity. Accordingly, authentic or resolute Dasein is the one which *repeats* traditional possibilities of existence without suppressing the truth of its Self and without being lost in public anonymity. Heidegger writes: "The authentic repetition of a possibility of existence that has been— the possibility that Dasein may choose its hero—is grounded existentially in anticipatory resoluteness (Heidegger, 1962: 437). Secondly, in order for Dasein, which listens to the call of its unquestioned public world in its everyday life, to hear the voice of its conscience correctly, know the truth of its Self, and, thus, become authentic, it needs to be provided with "the possibility of another kind of hearing" (Heidegger, 1962: 316). In order for this to happen, the unquestioned public world, as well as this world's naturalized norms, roles, standards, and ways of interpreting entities, must be problematized and denaturalized. Only then can Dasein have access to the truth of its Self and realize its historical contingency, performativity, and existential culpability. In short, authenticity requires that the "hardened tradition," one that "takes what has come down to us and delivers it over to self-evidence," must be "loosened up" (Heidegger, 1962: 43–44).

For Heidegger, it is authentic repetition that can loosen up this "hardened tradition." The reason is that authentic repetition has not only a "monumental" and "antiquarian," but also a "critical" aspect. On the one hand, authentic repetition refers to "the possibility of reverently preserving the existence that has-been-there," reverently preserving "the 'monumental' possibilities of human existence"—ones that have molded Dasein's world into its current form (Heidegger, 1962: 448). On the other hand, however, to reverently preserve does not amount to blindly imitating the past, but *re-appropriating* what has been handed down to Dasein *critically* and *creatively*, in order to *problematize* the calcified and naturalized status of what is taken for granted in Dasein's historical world. Heidegger writes: the authentic "repetition makes a *reciprocative rejoinder* to the possibility of that existence which has-been-there. But when such a rejoinder is made to this possibility [...] it is at the same time a *disavowal* of that which in the 'today' is working itself out as the 'past'" (Heidegger, 1962: 437–438).

The critical and creative aspects of repetition are the *sine qua non* for authenticity and freedom, because if the public world as the taken-for-granted context of meaning is not decalcified and denaturalized by critical and creative re-appropriations of the traditional possibilities, then what has been handed down to Dasein by the tradition becomes self-evident, functioning as something ahistorical and asocial, or as something natural and inevitable, such that the tradition becomes not a source from which Dasein can draw historically contingent guidelines to authentically compose its life, but the locus of anonymity, conformism, and lostness, alienating Dasein from the truth of its Self. In short, critically and creatively re-appropriating the traditional possibilities of existence in order to problematize what is taken for granted in the public world is a *spiritual exercise*, an *anxiety-engendering exercise*, that helps Dasein understand the truth of its Self and at the same time become authentic, which are the *sine qua non* for having access to the truth of Being.

Before concluding, it is worth noting that reading Heidegger's understanding of authentic repetition as a spiritual exercise may help us track down one line of continuity between his early philosophy and the so-called turn (*Kehre*) in his thought in the second half of the 1930s. For example, in his 1936 "The Origin of the Work of Art," Heidegger refers to genuine art-works as tools of authentic repetition. Specifically, for Heidegger, what makes art-works genuine is their functioning as building-stones on the way to the creation of a new world as a new context of meaning, within which entities become what they are thanks to this context's understanding of Being. In his words, genuine art-works "liberate the free space of the open region [i.e., clearing]," and "Beings can be as beings only if they stand within and stand out within what is cleared in this clearing" (Heidegger, 1993: 170, 178). However, this does not mean that genuine art-works create a new context of meaning *ex nihilo*. Instead, they *re-appropriate* what Gregory Fried calls the "historical givenness of meaning" or the traditional "givenness of the sense of Being" (Fried, 2000: 56, 61). In Heidegger's terminology, this means that the art-work "opens up a world and at the same time sets this world back again on earth" (Heidegger, 1993: 168). Nevertheless, just like the Heidegger of *Being and Time*, the Heidegger of the 1930s believes that re-appropriation does not refer to the blind imitation or restoration of the past. Instead, it has critical and creative, as well as decalcifying and denaturalizing aspects. He writes: "Repetition as we understand it is anything but the ameliorating continuation of what has been, by means of what has been"; it does not refer to "a new onset of mere restoration and uncreative imitation"; it "does not mean the stupid superficiality and impossibility of the mere occurrence of the *same* for a second and third time" (Heidegger, 2000: 41, 133; Heidegger, 2012: 45). Instead, "*to repeat and retrieve*" the tradition is to "conserve the familiar only in order to break out of it"; in short, it is to start "an upheaval and recreating of the customary," of what is calcified and naturalized to the point of preventing Dasein from self-knowledge, self-transformation, and having access to the truth of Being (Heidegger, 1994: 39; Heidegger, 2000: 41, 174).

It is also worth noting that, for Heidegger, the art-work is not the one and only tool of creatively re-appropriating the monumental possibilities of human existence. In his 1935 lecture-course, *Introduction to Metaphysics*, for example, Heidegger argues that "the work of the word as thinking" may have the same function as "the work of the word as poetry" and "the work of stone in temple and statue" (Heidegger, 2000: 204). That is, "genuine" philosophical works may also be interpreted as spiritual exercises, as anxiety-engendering authentic repetitions. Even though such an interpretation is beyond the scope of this chapter, it is possible to read Heidegger's philosophical *Seinsgeschichte* as a form of authentic repetition. Suffice it to say for the aim of this chapter that Heidegger introduces the term *Seinsgeschichte* in his 1936–1938 *Contributions to Philosophy*, where he problematizes the cultural paradigm of his time, specifically the paradigm of what he calls "the abandonment by being" and "machination"; but even before, as well as after, the introduction of this term, Heidegger *critically and creatively* interprets the major figures of the history of philosophy, especially Ancient Greek philosophy, in order to ask the question of Being (Heidegger, 2012). This means that it is possible to read Heidegger's obsession with Aristotle, Plato, and Pre-Socratics throughout his career, not as referring to his Aristotelianism or fascination by Pre-Socratics, but as an inevitable aspect of anxiety-engendering (philosophical–)spiritual exercises, aiming at critically and creatively re-appropriating the monumental possibilities of human existence, ones that have molded (Western, and Heidegger's) world into its current form, in order to problematize this world's taken-for-granted norms, standards, and ways of interpreting entities. As a result, just like his existential analytic of Dasein in *Being and Time*, Heidegger's later works may be regarded as instantiations of the tradition of spirituality, as spiritual exercises aiming at knowing and transforming one's Self in order to have access to the truth of Being with the aid of authentic repetitions.

Conclusion and the Politicization of Spirituality

I have argued that we can read Heidegger's early philosophy as a form of modern spirituality, and his *existential analytic of Dasein* as a spiritual exercise, which aims at the transformation of the subject/Dasein in order to have access to the truth (of the Self and of Being). I have also argued that such a reading may help us track down one line of continuity between Heidegger's early philosophy and the so-called turn in his thought in the second half of the 1930s. It is worth noting that reading Heidegger from the perspective of Foucault's interpretation of the tradition of spirituality may also help us come one step closer to understanding the relationship between Foucault and Heidegger, as well as uncovering the Heideggerian aspects of Foucault's understanding of resistance to political power. This is because Foucault argues that "an ethic of the self," *based on self-transformation*, is "an urgent, fundamental, and politically indispensable task," considering that "there is no first or final point of resistance to political power other than in the relationship one has to oneself" (Foucault, 2005: 252). For Foucault, self-transformation is the *sine qua non* for resistance to political power because power is productive. That is, the main function of power is not the suppression or rejection of the Self and its individuality, but the very production of it. In Foucault's words:

> The individual is not to be conceived as a sort of elementary nucleus, a primitive atom, a multiple and inert material on which power comes to fasten or against which it happens to strike, and in so doing subdues or crushes individuals. In fact, it is already one of the prime effects of power that certain bodies, certain gestures, certain discourses, certain desires, come to be identified and constituted as individuals. The individual, that is, is not the *vis-à-vis* of power; it is, I believe, one of its prime effects (Foucault, 1980; 98).

Moreover, just like Heidegger, Foucault believes that self-transformation cannot be accomplished without (genealogical) self-knowledge. The aim of Foucauldian genealogy is to have access to the truth of the Self. Specifically, it is to figure out how and through which historical mechanisms and power structures we are constructed as who we are, as "subjects of what we are doing, thinking, [and] saying," in order to determine what is historically contingent and, therefore, transformable in what we believe to be natural and inevitable in the Self (Foucault, 1997: 113). This is the reason why Foucault states "if I know the truth I will be changed," and argues that freedom lies in the possibility of such a change, namely in "the possibility of no longer being, doing, or thinking what we are, do, or think" (Foucault, 1989: 379; Foucault, 1997: 114). As a result, it is possible to read Foucault's philosophy as referring to the *politicization* of Heideggerian spirituality, though such a reading is beyond the scope of this chapter.

References

Fried, Gregory (2000). *Heidegger's Polemos: From Being to Politics*. New Haven: Yale University Press.

Foucault, Michel (1980). Two Lectures. In *Power/Knowledge: Selected Interviews and Other Writings, 1972–1977*. (C. Gordon, ed. Trans.). New York: Harvester Wheatsheaf.

Foucault, Michel (1988). The Return of Morality. In *Politics, Philosophy, Culture: Interviews and Other Writings, 1977–1984*. (L. Kritzman, Ed. & A. Sheridan, Trans.). London: Routledge.

Foucault, Michel (1989). An Ethics of Pleasure. In *Foucault Live: Interviews, 1961–1984*. (S. Lotringer, Ed. & L. Hochroth & J. Johnston, Trans.). New York: Semiotext(e).

Foucault, Michel (1997). What is Enlightenment? In *The Politics of Truth*. (S. Lotringer, Ed. & L. Hochroth & C. Porter, Trans.). New York: Semiotext(e).

Foucault, Michel (2005). *The Hermeneutics of the Subject: Lectures at the Collège de France, 1981–1982*. (A. Davidson, Ed. & G. Burchell, Trans.). New York: Palgrave Macmillan.

Guignon, Charles (1983). *Heidegger and the Problem of Knowledge*. Indiana: Hackett Publishing.

Guignon, Charles (1985). Heidegger's "Authenticity" Revisited. *The Review of Metaphysics* Vol. 38. No. 2. pp. 321–339.

Heidegger, Martin (1962). *Being and Time*. (J. Macquarrie & E. Robinson, Trans.). New York: Blackwell.

Heidegger, Martin (1982). *The Basic Problems of Phenomenology*. (A. Hofstadter, Trans.). Indiana: Indiana University Press.

Heidegger, Martin (1984). *The Metaphysical Foundations of Logic*. (M. Heim, Trans.). Indiana: Indiana University Press.

Heidegger, Martin (1993). The Origin of the Work of Art. In *Basic Writings*. (D. F. Krell, ed. Trans.). New York: Harper Perennial Publishing.

Heidegger, Martin (1994). *Basic Questions of Philosophy: Selected "Problems" of Logic*. (R. Rojcewicz & A. Schuwer, Trans.). Indiana: Indiana University Press.

Heidegger, Martin (1995). *The Fundamental Concepts of Metaphysics: World, Finitude, Solitude*. (W. McNeill & N. Walker, Trans.). Indiana: Indiana University Press.

Heidegger, Martin (2000). *Introduction to Metaphysics*. (G. Fried & R. Polt, Trans.). New Haven: Yale University Press.

Heidegger, Martin (2005). *The Essence of Human Freedom*. (T. Sadler, Trans.). New York: Continuum.

Heidegger, Martin (2012). *Contributions to Philosophy: Of the Event*. (R. Rojcewicz & D. Vallega-Neu, Trans.). Indiana: Indiana University Press.

Elif Çırakman

On the Ground of Law: Heidegger's Suspension of the Ethical and the Political

What is law? The significance and scope of this question for modernity are not only vaguely, but also widely understood. No matter how widely its scope is understood we dwell in the midst of this question. Thus we are continually confronted with its various meanings –moral, judicial, ethical, political, natural, positive, divine meanings of law. Accordingly, we can say that with respect to different conceptions of law, our conception of ourselves is defined. In our modern world, we define ourselves as legal persons, moral subjects, social agents, political actors, or as natural physical beings. In all these spheres, we understand the world and ourselves in a law-governed way. In this respect, we can claim that the question of law and the question of being-human imply each other, no matter how this implication is pursued in natural, moral, political or legal terms. Clearly to account for the nature of this implication in all these contexts is over and beyond the scope of this chapter. I shall rather focus on the question of the intelligibility of law for human beings, that is, the ways in which the ground of normativity appeals to us. In this respect, the fundamental questions of this paper are as follows: How does the relation between law and being-human unfold? What does it mean to be human given its relation to the law that it both submits and gives to itself? Furthermore, on what grounds can this relation be rendered intelligible?[1]

Here, my purpose is to respond these questions through the examination of Martin Heidegger's interpretation of Immanuel Kant in his *The Basic Problems of Phenomenology* and *Kant and the Problem of Metaphysics*. My reading aims to explore the Heideggerian configuration of the relation between law and being-human. To this purpose, I shall first focus on Heidegger's interpretation of Kant's notion of respect for the moral law in order to lay stress upon the finitude that our freedom assumes, which discloses the primordial ontological question, i.e.,

---

1   See for an extensive study of these questions in the works of Kant, Heideger, and Levinas the unpublished Ph.D. dissertation defended in 2001 at Middle East Technical University in the Department of Philosophy, Ankara; Elif Çırakman, *The Ground of Law and Being-Human: a Kantian Antinomy and its Repercussions in Heidegger and Levinas*. Ankara, METU (2001).

the question of being (*Sein*) that Kant seems to suppress. In his analysis of the Kantian notion of respect, i.e. our rational susceptibility to the command of the moral law, Heidegger questions the possibility of moral resolution in its relation to our finitude which inevitably requires a more radical understanding of sensibility and a more original understanding of time and temporality. Then, with a brief reference to *Being and Time*, we shall be able to see the radical transformation of the Kantian understanding of moral resolution, i.e. autonomy, into Heidegger's elaboration of "anticipatory resoluteness" within which we can discern the ground of our susceptibility to the call of conscience, i.e. authenticity, as ultimately without a ground or reason, but as always already unfolding in the historical existence of *Dasein*. As I shall point, the authenticity of *Dasein* turns out to be eventually a matter of finding oneself in terms of the destiny of the hero without an assumed destination.

Above all, in the following, I seek to analyze how Heidegger gives response to the question of the ground of law by inquiring into the question of being-human in his early thinking. I shall argue that Heidegger's suspension of the ethical and the political questions in his reading of Kant is a way to delve deeper into the ground of normativity that is constitutive of our being-human. This, as I shall inspect, is the most pressing issue in his confrontation with Kant and with what the Kantian critical philosophy represents in the modern philosophy. Finally, in the conclusion, I shall just point to the way in which Heidegger, in his later thinking, transformed the whole issue into a more radical ground in terms of the history of being within which we find ourselves with the task of instituting its truth without any final accomplishment. In his later thinking, as I shall claim, the ground of law turns out to be a matter of finding ourselves in and through the destination of being which is without a destiny. Here, unlike his early thinking, the course of questioning has changed. Heidegger now seems to give response to the question of being-human by inquiring into to the question of the ground of law which consists in "the dispensation (*die Schickung*) of being" (Heidegger, 1978: 216).

The Question of the Ground of Law

The Kantian turning point in modern philosophy presents the ground of law as rationality. In the *Critique of Pure Reason*, Kant sets the stage for pure reason in its theoretical employment, that is, in its law-setting function –putting laws together with one another. In the *Critique of Practical Reason*, pure reason, in its practical employment, is elaborated in its law-giving function. Thus Kant's conception of law has both a theoretical and a practical ground. These two distinct grounds of law indicate, in turn, two distinct characters of our rationality. On the one hand, we are *finite* in our law-setting capacity. On the other hand, we are claimed to be *free* in our law-giving capacity. In the Kantian account, the unity of pure reason or, in other words, the unity of the ground of law remains a serious problem. For one thing, Kant understands the notion of ground in terms of causality. Since he inspects the causality of nature within the theoretical employment of pure reason, and the causality of freedom within its practical employment, he ends up with two sorts of causality, i.e. two separate grounds. This, I claim, is the Kantian problem which Heidegger tries to overcome.

For one thing, we should admit that Heidegger does not explicitly deal with the question of law. However, this does not mean that he ignores the question. Rather, he carries the ground of this question to an ontological plane. Heidegger understands the notion of *ground* not in terms of the causality of a cause, but rather in terms of the *being* (*Sein*) of beings. Thus, as we shall see, the Heideggerian turning point in philosophy inspects the ground of law in the verbal sense of "being" (*Sein*). I define the Kantian predicament, i.e. the problem of "the antinomy of law", as the necessity of two equally compelling but conflicting claims about the ground of law as revealing the double character of our subjectivity. In the following, I elaborate the repercussions of the Kantian antinomy –of the laws of nature and the laws of freedom– with respect to the problem of the interpretation of subjectivity which is the touchstone of modern metaphysics.[2] I claim that the initiative of Heidegger's central occupation with the being of human existence (*Dasein*) and with the question of being (*Sein*) is his reflection on Kant's antinomy. Thus, in order for Heidegger to introduce *Dasein* as the originary reference for his thinking, he has to overcome the modern metaphysics of subjectivity by confronting its antinomies.

---

2   Gillian Rose, in *Dialectic of Nihilism*, qualifies this activity and passivity of the subject that Heidegger examines as the antinomy of law because she claims that "this dual status is legal status as such, according to which the subject is active, 'the subject of the law', and passive, 'subjected to the law.'" Accordingly, she concludes that this "antinomical history of the subject is the Event (*das Ereignis*)" (Rose, 1984: 65). Rose explains the Heideggerian notion, i.e. the event, as follows: "*Das Ereignis* is the historical event, qualitative time, what happens (historic presence), another word for happening, *Das Geschehen*, which is modified in *die Geschichte*, 'history'". *Das Ereignis* also includes the adjective/verb, *eigen/eignen* – "own", "to make one's own". The prefix "*er*" transforms the imperfect verb, one that expresses a continuous or lasting state, condition or process, into a perfect one, marked by a beginning and an end. Hence, "*ereignen*" connotes identity without representation, property without having, and completion without reflection of a point in time" (Rose, 1984: 58).

The antinomy of modern metaphysics of subjectivity gains its overflow from the double determination of the term "subject". On the one hand, the subject is a *subjectum*, i.e., an individual substance or a material substratum, but on the other hand, it is a *subjectus*, i.e., a political and a juridical term that refers to subjection and submission. The translation of the Greek *hypokeimenon* into Latin *subjectum* indicates the meaning of subject as something "thrown under", as "that which is constantly present in every presencing" (Rose, 1984: 62–65). The subjectivity of the subject assumes itself as opposed to the object. Therefore, it is the source of the oppositions of "subject and object", or "persons and things". This event also points to the equation of man and the subject, and raises the question of its right as to knowledge and as to action, i.e. *de jure* man. The question of *subjectus* is forgotten or, in other words, it is interiorized in the constitution of subjectivity as the self-submission of the subject. All these developments of the term "subject" find its achievement in Kant's metaphysics of subjectivity and, particularly, in his metaphysics of morals. In this respect, Heidegger's confrontation with Kant is significant, which also sheds a light on Heidegger's fundamental questions, i.e., "What is the meaning of being (*Sein*) in general?", and "How is the understanding of being possible?" (Heidegger, 1988: 19). Therefore, in order to understand the ground of these questions, i.e. the possibility of a fundamental ontology, it is significant first to investigate Heidegger's relation to the Kantian understanding of subjectivity.

Heidegger regards Kant as a turning point in the history of philosophy bringing forth a new twist to the interpretation of subject's subjectivity. Heidegger's critical examination of Kant proposes the de-construction and the appropriation of the history of philosophy by correcting the orientation to the subject which leads him to the elaboration of the existential constitution of *Dasein* and its comportment to being (*Sein*). In this respect, I will explore Heidegger's path of thinking which leads us to a reflection of the being of human existence - *Dasein* as the openness to being (*Sein*). This exploration will, hopefully, provide a hint for the reason why Heidegger did not directly occupy himself with the philosophical problems of law, ethics and politics.

For one thing, it should be admitted that Heidegger never raises explicitly the question of the relation between being-human and law. However, in *Kant and the Problem of Metaphysics*, he claims that the problem of finitude cannot be addressed without the question "what does law mean here, and how is the lawfulness itself constitutive for *Dasein* and for the personality?" (Heidegger, 1997: 196–197). Hence, he questions the inner function of the law –the imperative– for *Dasein* by exploring the ways in which it refers to the finitude in

Dasein.[3] His suspension of ethical and political inquiry rests on his conviction concerning the necessity of a more primordial understanding of "who" *Dasein* is. With regard to this, I argue that his suspension does not seem to be a strict abolition of the ethical and political questions, but rather an attempt to locate them into the context of the primordial relationship between *Dasein* and being (*Sein*). This displacement of ethical and political thinking back into the question of the relation between *Dasein* and being (*Sein*) eventually brings forth a new configuration of the relation between the meaning of law and being-human. In this context, one can also question the ways in which this new configuration radicalizes the Kantian antinomy of law.

Finitude and Freedom: Analysis of the Kantian Notion of Respect

Kant's aim to lay a ground for metaphysics is one of the main concerns of Heidegger's early thinking. For one thing, Heidegger's occupation with Kant and the problem of metaphysics indicates a deconstructive retrieval of Kant's transcendental philosophy. Hence, this retrieval can be regarded as pushing the limits of transcendental philosophy up to its end by delimiting its inner possibility. Heidegger interprets the Kantian ground-laying as the disclosure of the inner possibility of ontology. His deconstructive reading leads him to make explicit what remains hidden in Kant's approach. It is the essential meaning of human finitude inherent in human pure reason. For Heidegger, the resolution of the Kantian problem resides in showing the possibility of the unity of human existence – of the *being* of human existence as a whole. We are bound *to be*. Our mode of being (*Sein*) consists in our understanding of the being we are. This indicates our *freedom* to be. However, we are also bound to be *finite*. This indicates our *finite freedom*, which is our essential unfolding in the world as temporal.

In this deconstructive retrieval, Heidegger interprets the meaning of the "transcendental" as forming (*bilden*) the horizon within which the beings manifest themselves. For Heidegger, this horizon is always based on our pre-understanding of being (*Sein*). What is distinctive of human reason must be its stepping-over to meet its objects. This "stepping-over" of pure reason is what Heidegger calls as "transcendence" (*Überstieg*), and the essence of transcendence characterizes the understanding of being (Heidegger, 1997: 10–11). In

---

3   See Heidegger (1997), "Davos Disputation between Ernst Cassirer and Martin Heidegger" in Appendix IV.

this regard, transcendence is the condition of the possibility of transcendental knowledge taking place in the horizon of time.

In Heidegger's ontological account, the problem of transcendence is now transformed into a question of the possible unity of human freedom and finitude. Heidegger's account of what it means to be human in terms of *Dasein* brings the question of being into a new horizon by exploring its relation to time. In other words, Heidegger interprets time as forming the unity of the essential unfolding of human existence. In this respect, he tries to overcome the Kantian distinctions such as the distinction between the empirical and the intelligible character, the distinction between metaphysics of nature and of morality, the distinction between theoretical and practical reason, within the scope of human finitude (Heidegger, 1997: 132). For one thing, these Kantian distinctions are all intended as a means for the resolution of the problem – the reconciliation of freedom and natural necessity. Then, we can ask whether Heidegger's project of overcoming the Kantian distinctions would not lead us back to the core of the problem, that is, the sense of finitude in the self-legislative character of the subject. Heidegger, in his interpretation of Kant, inspects the sense of finitude through an analysis of the Kantian notion of respect for the moral law.

In Kant's philosophy, the true characterization of subjectivity finds its expression in the moral personality of human being. Thus moral personality distinguishes one as a responsible and accountable moral subject. The moral personality is a specific mode of self-consciousness, that is, moral self-consciousness (Heidegger, 1988: 132). However, this new modification of self-consciousness is different from the empirical and transcendental ones. Moral self-consciousness, or moral personality, is the personality *proper* as the most appropriate determination belonging to one's true being in the sense that it is the power of moral resolution which makes possible the elevation of one's rational nature by means of his/her acting as an intelligible cause and, therefore, displays his/her "higher vocation" as an autonomous moral person (Kant, 1956: 90).

Human beings, in fact, both have a sensuous and a rational nature, and in that sense, being-human is conditioned by the double structure of human existence, that is, the empirical and the intelligible character of our being. Because of this double structure, morality is possible, and an incentive to morality is necessary and required. This receptivity to the thought of duty or, in other words, moral resolution has its origin in the effectiveness of pure practical reason which has an influence on the sensibility of the subject by the moral law (Kant, 1956: 78). When practical reason rejects all the rival claims of inclination –the claims of self-regard that consist of selfishness and self-conceit– it gives authority and sovereignty to the law. (Kant, 1956: 76, 79). The work of practical reason lies in calling to notice the purity of the will.

Admittedly, the relation between man and law is an internal relation of the divided self since the origin of constraint is nothing other than one's own legislative reason which imposes its authority on the sensuous nature of the self. This divided selfhood achieves its unity when it *freely* submits its will to a law of its own. This requires on the part of the self the *resoluteness* "to prefer the law to everything else merely out of respect for it" (Kant, 1956: 155). This relation is formulated in the second part of *Critique of Practical Reason* called "Methodology of Pure Practical Reason". What "methodology" means for Kant is "the way in which we can secure to the laws of pure practical reason access to the human mind and an influence on its maxims", or in other words it is "the way we can make the objectively practical reason also subjectively practical" (Kant, 1956: 155). The mediating term is the respect for law, i.e., the thought of duty. For Kant, the purpose of methodology is to show that in human rationality, that is, in the independence of man's intelligible nature, there is this receptivity to the thought of duty where it is "the strongest incentive to the good" (Kant, 1956: 155,156). The resoluteness to prefer the law to everything else merely out of respect is the property of human mind (Kant, 1956: 155,156). Kant justifies this statement as follows: "if human nature were not so constituted, no way of presenting the law by circumlocutions and indirect recommendations could ever produce morality of intentions" (Kant, 1956: 155). Therefore it would be impossible to feel respect for the law if it were possible completely to free oneself from reason in judging (Kant, 1956: 156). However, it is not possible to detach oneself completely from rationality, and this is the reason why respect "is a tribute we cannot refuse to pay to merit whether we will or not; we can indeed outwardly withhold it, but we cannot help feeling it inwardly" (Kant, 1956: 80).

The feeling of respect is produced by an intellectual cause and, in this respect, it sustains the consciousness of freedom. Kant claims that in instances of pure moral resolutions, what is revealed to man is "a faculty of inner freedom to release himself from the impetuous importunity of the inclinations" (Kant, 1956: 165). Moral resoluteness is the consciousness of freedom. Thus, in moral resolution, one is not subjected to the causality of empirical-sensuous nature, but is obedient to an intelligible law that has its origin nowhere else than in the pure practical reason. Thus Kant says that human beings are indeed "legislative members of a moral realm which is possible through freedom and which is presented to us as an object of respect by practical reason" (Kant, 1956: 85). However, because they are at the same time subjects in it, the moral law for finite human beings is "a law of duty, of moral constraint and of the determination of his actions through respect for the law and reverence for its duty" (Kant, 1956: 85). Therefore, moral resoluteness, or in other words, authenticity requires both the autonomy (self-legislation) and the finitude of human beings. Kant's account of the respect for the moral law discloses human condition as both autonomous and finite.

In the moral self-consciousness, with regard to its distinction as the personality proper, the true being of subjectivity must be revealed to oneself. But, how is this revealing possible? Heidegger claims that this revealing of oneself pertains to the essential nature of feeling: "not only that it is feeling *for* something but also that this feeling for something at the same time makes feelable the feeler himself and his state, his being in the broadest sense" (Heidegger, 1988: 132). Accordingly now, the question should be the possibility of a feeling which is not sensible at all. Thus, the possibility of a moral feeling can be the only condition that gives the determination of what is distinct in moral subject, i.e. the moral feeling, which is "making manifest of the ego in its non-sensible character, a revealing of itself as an acting being" (Heidegger, 1988: 133). For one thing, respect *for* the law is the only way in which the moral law approaches the moral subject and, simultaneously, it is the only way in which the moral self feels its own self (Heidegger, 1988: 135). In other words, this moral feeling reveals that which it feels and the self who feels. In this regard, on the one hand, it is the specific revelation of the moral law since it is the feeling *for* the law. On the other hand, it is the specific revelation of the moral subject, since it is the self-feeling in this having-feeling-for the law. How does the respectful self in the moral feeling of respect manifest to itself? In Heidegger's words:

> In respect for the law, I submit myself to the law. The specific having of a feeling for the law which is present in respect is a self-subjection. I subject myself in respect for the law to my own self as the free self. In this subjection of myself I am manifest to myself; I am as I myself. The question is, as what or, more precisely, as *who?* (Heidegger, 1988: 135)

In submitting myself to the law, I subject myself to myself *as pure reason* because this feeling of respect is produced by pure reason. Therefore, in this self-subjection, the self that is respectful manifests itself as pure reason, i.e. as the free self-determining being. In other words, as pure reason, I give myself the law. My subjection to the law is only a self-subjection through which I recognize my free and self-determining being –the true being of my subjectivity is revealed to me for the first time in this moral feeling of respect (Heidegger, 1988: 135). This self-subjection is a self-elevation since now the self is transparent to itself in its true being. In the elevation of the submissive self to the free self, one is disclosed to oneself in his/her dignity which is to have respect for oneself. For one thing, in having-feeling-for the law which I give to myself in the sense of self-subjection,

I have a feeling for myself, i.e. self-feeling. Therefore, I am revealed to myself in my absolute worth, that is, in my ownmost dignity. As Heidegger claims,

> Respect is the mode of the ego's being-with-itself (*Bei-sich-selbst-sein*) according to which it does not disparage the hero in its soul. The moral feeling, as respect for the law, is nothing but the self's being responsible to itself and for itself. This moral feeling is a distinctive way in which the ego understands itself as ego directly, purely, and free of all sensuous determination. (Heidegger, 1988: 135–6)

Accordingly, the immediate determination of the subject by the law through the feeling of respect reveals its *authenticity* as its true being which is the mode of becoming self-manifest in one's ownmost dignity. Heidegger interprets "respect" as self-responsibility because in this feeling consists the basic structure of giving response to oneself. Accordingly, the subject knows itself not in a general sense as the knowledge of an ego in general, that is, not as passive, but as active, that is, as a responsible self where its self is revealed to itself in its activity (Heidegger, 1988: 137). The self knows its ego *actively* in the sense that "I myself *am* –am *acting*", "as in each case mine, the ego as in each case the individual factical ego" (Heidegger, 1988: 137).

In *The Basic Problems of Phenomenology*, Heidegger claims that practical self-consciousness in the sense of respect constitutes the moral personality, the personality proper. However, at this stage of his analysis, he puts forward a fundamental distinction between the ontical and the ontological. In order to clarify this distinction, he formulates the following question: "Given that in the above described way the self is revealed *ontically* in the moral feeling of respect as being an ego, how is that self to be defined *ontologically*?" (Heidegger, 1988: 137).[4] Heidegger regards the moral feeling of respect as the ontical manifestation of the factically existent ego. For one thing, although Kant never poses this distinction between the ontical and the ontological, Heidegger claims that in the ontical exposition of the self, the possibility of its ontological constitution is inherent. In this respect, he sets himself the task of exploring the ontological concept of moral personality in Kant.

---

4   The ontological difference is a difference between being (*Sein*) and beings (*Seiende*), that which 'is'. The former designates that which is ontological, the latter that which is ontical. By ontical Heidegger means that which is concerned primarily with entities in the factual level. Whereas, by ontological, he means the deep structures that underlie the ontic, the being of entities. In the final analysis, Heidegger asserts that being (*Sein*) is not an entity itself, and for the philosophy proper, they must be distinguished.

The ontological meaning of person is found in Kant's second formulation of the categorical imperative, that is, in the definition of person as an end-in-itself. Thus, this ontological characterization of person is inherent in the moral feeling of respect, since "in respect, in acting ethically, man makes himself" by *making* himself his own end (Heidegger, 1988: 137–8). In making himself his own end, and thus in existing objectively as an end, but never merely as a means, a person differentiates itself from things. This difference designates the concept of humanity as the essence of human, which enables Kant to formulate the second formulation of the categorical imperative. What is revealed in this imperative is "the proper ought-to-be of man", and it "prescribes what man can be as defined by the essential nature of his existence" (Heidegger, 1988: 139). This principle also reveals *the realm of ends, the being-with-one-another*, and *the commercium of persons* as such. For Heidegger, the kingdom of ends signifies, in its ontical sense, being-with-one-another of the factically existing persons themselves (Heidegger, 1988: 139).

Heidegger regards the ontological constitution of the person in its being an end-in-itself. The *commercium* of free beings designates the kingdom of ends which is specifically the moral relation among persons as ends in themselves. Ends, or purposes, must be taken in an ontical sense, as an existent end which is an existing person. This determination sets the limit for arbitrary choice and signifies the nature of person as freedom (Heidegger, 1988: 138). For one thing, this *commercium* or kingdom in the Kantian sense ensures a specific relation among persons. This specific relation manifests the personality of person as an object of respect, that is, as a thing (*Ding*) whose existence is an end in itself. Because the nature of person is determined as an object of respect, it is also determined as freedom. In this respect the realm of ends (*being-with-one-another*) is the realm of freedom (Heidegger, 1988: 138–9).

In *The Basic Problems of Phenomenology*, Heidegger further argues as follows:

> It should be noted that finite substances, things (*Sachen*) as well as persons, are not simply extant in any arbitrary way, but exist in reciprocity, in a *commercium*. This reciprocal action is founded on causality, which Kant takes to be the faculty of producing effects. In correspondence with the basic ontological distinction between things and persons he distinguishes a double causality: causality of nature and causality of freedom. (Heidegger, 1988: 148)

At this stage, Heidegger confronts directly with Kant's treatment of the third antinomy of pure reason, i.e. the double causality of nature and freedom. Kant tries to solve the antinomy of law by distinguishing the manner of being in the *commercium* of finite beings. Although *commercium* signifies a sort of bringing together of beings in their reciprocal action, it becomes in this context the division founded on causality. On the one hand, the subject-ego exists actively in the *commercium* of free beings under the causality of freedom, since the will is able to start a series of causes. On the other hand, the subject-ego exists passively in the *commercium* of things, that is, as subjected to the causality of nature. The causality of freedom is manifested in the *commercium* of free beings as spontaneous intelligences comprehending themselves in their activity. They come to "know" themselves in their active responsibility that signifies freedom. Thus, the moral law for which we have respect is the form of an intellectual causality, i.e. the causality of freedom. As a spontaneous intelligence, I am "the *subject* of law", a subjective genitive in the sense of the "initiator" or the "author" of law. Then, the subject as pure practical reason is the intelligible ground of law acting as an intelligible cause. It is only in this respect that the moral subject practically "knows" itself as an active intelligible cause, that is, as free. Thus, in subjecting myself to the law, I subject myself to myself as pure reason. In this sense, I raise myself to myself as a self-determining free being (Heidegger, 1988: 135). However, I am at the same time "subjected to the law", that is, "law's subject", the objective and the possessive genitive. In this respect, Heidegger claims that "man is at once master and servant of himself" (Heidegger, 1988: 137).

The problem of modern metaphysics resides in its separation of a subject from an object that implies a transcendent sphere (Heidegger, 1988: 64). Heidegger tries to solve this problem of subject-object relation by claiming, unlike Kant, that the " '*commercium*' of the subject with a world does not get *created* for the first time by knowing, nor does it *arise* from some way in which the world acts upon a subject" (Heidegger, 1962: 90). Instead, the being that we ourselves are always already within this *commercium*, which enables us to interpret, to know, to project, to act, and to relate with the beings that we ourselves are not. The crucial point, which Heidegger tries to accomplish, is the primordiality of being-in-the-world. Hence, the world is the dwelling place in which the disclosure of being (the ontological truth) and the manifestness of beings (the ontical truth) are first possible. In this regard, the truth of being and of beings requires a place in order to disclose itself. This place is a matter of "openness" (*Da*) in the sense of clearing (*Lichtung*), i.e. the openness of the world (*Welt*). Heidegger's essential criticism against Kant resides in the fact that Kant's treatment of the antinomies of pure reason undermines the ontological possibilities inherent in the notions of time and world. In Heidegger's words, "Kant did not see the phenomenon of the world" (Heidegger, 1962: 368).

> In everyday terms, we understand ourselves and our existence by way of the activities we pursue and the things we take care of. We understand ourselves by starting from them because the Dasein finds itself primarily in things. The Dasein does not need a special kind of observation, nor does it need to conduct a sort of espionage on the ego in order to have the self; rather, as the Dasein gives itself immediately and passionately to the world itself, its own self is reflected to it from things. (Heidegger, 1988: 159)

Dasein's giving itself to the world immediately and passionately signifies its being-always-already-in-the-world. This signifies an elementary phenomeno-logical fact of existence, which should be taken into account before any talk about the subject-object relation. Thus, this factuality of existence surpasses the significance of subject-object relation through its primodiality and unity. The self of the *Dasein* is *there* before any reflection and before any subject-object division. This means that *Dasein* has always submitted and committed itself to the "there". In this submission of itself to "there", the self of *Dasein* is given to itself. At this stage, I would like to claim that *Dasein's* submission to the world revives the meaning of subject as *subjectus*, indicating a political and juridical term that refers to subjection and submission. Primordially, *Dasein* is not the *subjectum,* but the *subjectus.* Heidegger retrieves this forgotten meaning of the term in order to overcome and correct the orientation modern metaphysics toward the *subjectum.* In *Being and Time,* he says that "Dasein, in so far as it *is,* has always submitted itself already to a "world" which it encounters, and this *submission* belongs essentially to its Being" (Heidegger, 1962: 120–121). The German term for "submission" that Heidegger uses is *Angewiesenheit,* and it is the past parti-ciple of *Anwiesenheit* (assignment) so it often takes the connotation of "being dependent on" something or even "at mercy" of something.[5] This original sub-mission of *Dasein* to the world is prior to the duality of subject and object, and of person and thing (*Sache*), and in fact, it is the ground within which these distinctions are possible.

The Unity of Pure Reason: The Original Time

Above all, for Heidegger, the possibility of transcendence carries the implication of human finitude. Thus, Heidegger prepares the ground for the elucidation of the question of transcendence and of finitude as follows:

> This going-beyond to the "wholly other," however, requires a Being-in-there (*Darinnensein*), in a "medium" within which this "wholly other" – that the knowing creature itself is not and over which it is not the master – can be encountered. (Heidegger, 1997: 82)

---

5   See (Heidegger, 1962: 121) translator's note.

In *Kant and the Problem of Metaphysics*, Heidegger regards the possibility of this "medium" in a genuine understanding of time. This medium, as the possibility of transcendence, makes possible the understanding of being. The true being of the self can only be made manifest within this medium.

In *Kant and the Problem of Metaphysics*, Heidegger interprets respect before the law as "in itself a making-manifest of myself as acting self", or in other words, as "the manner of the Being-its-self of the I (*des Selbstseins des Ich*)" (Heidegger, 1997: 111). For Heidegger, respect designates "the manner of the self's Being responsible, face to face with itself", which is nothing other than self's authentic Being-its-self (Heidegger, 1997: 111). This moral *feeling* of respect is, in fact, the "feeling of my existence" (Heidegger, 1997: 112). Thus, in addition to the consciousness of law, this feeling *gives* simultaneously the consciousness of the self (Heidegger, 1997: 112). Heidegger explores the question of this manifestness of the self to itself, i.e. this self-disclosure, as a matter of raising the question of "who" within the possibility of *pure sensible reason*.

The possibility of pure sensible reason resides in the unity of the spontaneity and the receptivity of the subject. Thus, it indicates the unity of the activity and the passivity of the subject. Heidegger claims that the subject's self-submitting, immediate surrender to the law is pure receptivity, whereas the free self-affecting of the law is pure spontaneity (Heidegger, 1997: 112). Accordingly, it is through the original unity, or springing-forth of the pure receptivity and the pure spontaneity that the moral self-consciousness emerges. Heidegger inspects this original unity by reinterpreting the function of transcendental imagination in Kant. In this respect, Heidegger quite controversially traces the delimiting condition of the moral self-consciousness back to the transcendental power of imagination (Heidegger, 1997: 109). Hence, Heidegger tries to disclose the origin of practical reason in the temporalizing activity of transcendental power of imagination signifying finitude, although Kant warns us against any attempt to contaminate suprasensible moral law with imagination and intuition, that is, with anything that pertains to sensibility (Heidegger, 1997: 109).

Controversially this delimitation originates an account of pure sensuous practical reason that is simultaneously receptive and spontaneous. In this regard, Heidegger attributes a moral dimension to receptivity. Hence, it is through the rational feeling of respect for law –self-affecting affection or self-submissive submission– that we receive the moral principles that constitutes our duty. Heidegger's main concern is to explore how morality is rooted in the temporal and what this temporality means to be. Here, the transcendental power of imagination is significant because of its temporalizing function.

The problem that Heidegger focuses on is the possibility of reconciling moral freedom and human finitude. The central question for Heidegger is that given the unconditioned character of the moral law, how it is possible to conceive human freedom within a temporal perspective. In other words, the problem is the possibility of pure sensible reason which is over and beyond the double character of human existence. The transcendental imagination, as the faculty of time-formation, and its import for the practical reason are of vital significance for Heidegger to deal with this central question.

Heidegger regards the transcendental power of imagination as the original ground of the possibility of human subjectivity in its unity and wholeness (Heidegger, 1997: 121). Thus, he claims that transcendental power of imagination as original pure synthesis lets a manifold to be intuited. Heidegger characterizes this synthesis as time-forming (Heidegger, 1997: 126). It is in this respect that the horizon of objects –the understanding of being– is first formed by the transcendental power of imagination which, for Heidegger, is the root of transcendence in disclosing the being (*Sein*) of the self and of beings (Heidegger, 1997: 97, 98). Hence, Heidegger argues as follows:

> The imagination forms the look of the horizon of objectivity as such in advance, before the experience of being. This look-forming (*Anblickbilden*) in the pure image (*Bilde*) of time, however, is not just prior to this or to that experience of the being, but rather always in advance, prior to any possible (experience). (Heidegger, 1997: 92)

Time is a form of pure intuition. Time forms the horizon within which the affections of senses strike us. Thus, it activates itself with what is intuited, which is first formed in it (Heidegger, 1997: 132). Moreover, since time is an *intuition*, it is the pure receptivity of what gives itself (Heidegger, 1997: 122). For one thing, what gives itself is not something at hand or present. For then its reception would be an empirical intuition. Rather, what gives itself is the look of the "now" (Heidegger, 1997: 122). What Heidegger means by the look of the "now" is the horizon that constitutes the "now" as within the looking ahead of its "coming-at-any-minute" and looking back on its "having-just-arrived" (Heidegger, 1997: 122). Time gives itself in its unity thanks to the unifying function of the transcendental power of imagination and, in this respect, "it prepares the look of succession from out of itself" as the pure affection of itself (Heidegger, 1997: 132). Heidegger argues that since the transcendental power of imagination allows time to spring forth by its original unifying function, it is nothing other than the original time (Heidegger, 1997: 131). What Heidegger means by the "original time" is the pure self-affection of time regarded as the original ground of transcendence (Heidegger, 1997: 140). If transcendence is defined at this stage as the understanding of being, then the original time provides the horizon of being within which understanding moves.

Heidegger claims that pure intuition, i.e. time, is a spontaneous receptivity. It is pure and spontaneous in the sense that it activates itself from out of itself. However, it is also purely receptive, in the sense that it is a pure taking-in-stride, that is, the capacity to be affected in the absence of experience independently of an immediate reference to an object. The problem is now to show how this pure intuition is in an original unity with pure thinking (apperception), which Heidegger characterizes as a receptive spontaneity. Hence, for Heidegger, this unity constitutes the unified essence of a finite, pure, sensible reason (Heidegger, 1997: 137). This is the most challenging interpretation of Kant that is given by Heidegger. Heidegger, himself, is aware of the fact that he introduces an interpretation, which is against the Kantian understanding of pure reason. Thus, he asks as follows: "How in general is pure thinking, the I of pure apperception, to have a temporal character when Kant opposes in the sharpest terms the "I think" in particular and reason in general to all time-relations?" (Heidegger, 1997: 128)

Let us see how he justifies the pure sensible reason which is the ground of human finitude. Recall that time necessarily affects the concept of representations of objects (Heidegger, 1997: 133). Heidegger interprets the horizon of objectivity in general as "the condition for the possibility of object (*Gegenstand*) with respect to its being-able-to-stand-against (*Gegenstehenkönnes*)" (Heidegger, 1997: 83). This horizon is in fact the horizon of finitude and transcendence at the same time. Time-forming function of transcendental imagination and its synthesis of the representations are nothing other than a matter of holding-open the horizon within which the being of the beings becomes discernible (Heidegger, 1997: 87). Being is unveiled and beings manifest themselves only within the horizon of original time that is understood as pure self affection. Therefore, the root of transcendence consists in being open to this unveiled being and the manifestness of beings. This transcendence is made possible through the pure self-affection of time accompanying all our representations by its synthetic activity, whereas the unity of its synthesis depends on the unity of apperception, i.e. the pure "I think" (Heidegger, 1997: 82). Heidegger searches the origin of the pure thinking in the transcendental power of imagination. In this respect, he claims not only that the pure thinking is spontaneous, but it is also receptive owing to the fact that "this original 'thinking' is pure imagining" (Heidegger, 1997: 106). Heidegger argues that this sense of free, forming, projecting thinking is in kinship with the transcendental power of imagination (Heidegger, 1997: 108). This is to say that pure thinking involves pure intuition, and it is itself a receptive spontaneity (Heidegger, 1997: 108). However, here intuition should not be understood as receiving what is given by a sense-organ. Heidegger extends the restricted sense that Kant allocates to sensibility. Heidegger interprets sensibility as the mark of our finitude, that is, as our rootedness in time. Therefore sensibility is regarded not only as the capacity to be affected by a sensible appearance, but also as ontologically, in terms of our capacity to be open to the manifestness of beings and the disclosure of being (*Sein*). It is in this sense that sensibility and understanding of being (*Sein*) are closely connected since sensibility provides the horizon for understanding which is primordially temporal. Pure sensibility, i.e. time, not only exhibits the possibility of disclosure and reception of beings within its self-affected horizon, but also provides the disclosure of the self.

Hence, Heidegger states that since "in its innermost essence the self is originally time itself, the 'I' cannot be grasped as 'temporal', i.e., as within time" (Heidegger, 1997: 136). Thus, the original time exhibits the finitude of human subjectivity in its wholeness. Finally, Heidegger argues for the possibility of interpreting pure reason as pure sensible reason. This interpretation displays the unity of pure sensibility and pure reason as follows:

> In this way, however, it is obvious at a glance that time as pure self-affection is not found "in the mind" "along with" pure apperception. Rather, as the ground for the possibility of selfhood, time already lies within pure apperception, and so it first makes the mind into a mind.
> Time and the "I think" no longer stand incompatibly and incomparably at odds; they are the same. With his laying of the ground for metaphysics, and through the radicalism with which, for the first time, he transcendentally interpreted both time, always for itself, and the "I think," always for itself, Kant brought both of them together in their original sameness – without, to be sure, expressly seeing this as such for himself. (Heidegger, 1997: 134)

What Heidegger means by the pure sensible reason is that the pure self-consciousness, in its innermost essence, is in unity with time as pure sensibility. Heidegger argues that, in the first edition of "Transcendental Deduction", Kant had seen the possible unity of grounding sources of mind, namely, sensibility and understanding in a third faculty that is the transcendental power of imagination. However, as Heidegger argues, Kant had to shrink back from this ground-laying in the second edition. Thus, Kant regards the transcendental power of imagination as not strong enough to delimit the subjectivity of the subject as a whole. In this context, the separation of original time and pure self-consciousness leads to the gap between empirical and intelligible realms and, in fact, to the gap between theoretical and practical reason.

Heidegger sees the possibility of the unity of reason in the original but concealed possibilities of Kant's account of transcendental power of imagination.

In this respect, he retrieves these concealed possibilities by his understanding of original time which is regarded as the origin of both theoretical and practical reason. Since the origin of pure self-consciousness resides in the transcendental power of imagination, then the origin of pure moral self-consciousness must also reside in this transcendental power (Heidegger, 1997: 109). The origin of practical reason, like that of theoretical reason, is the union between receptivity and spontaneity. It is a union that is sustained through imagination. However, as Llewelyn suggests, imagination is doubly ambiguous; on the one hand, with respect to theoretical reason, it is ambiguous as between sensibility and understanding, but on the other hand, with respect to practical reason, it is ambiguous as between feeling and reason (Llewelyn, 2000: 7). Hence, Heidegger tries to overcome this doubly ambiguous sense of imagination by searching the coincidence of these so-called opposite poles. Insofar as he can show how pure moral self-consciousness is receptive, it is possible for him to argue for a pure sensible reason. He finds this possibility in the moral feeling of respect through which the moral law is accessible to us.

Kant argues that respect is the only rational feeling. Obviously, he accepts that reason and feeling comes together in the respect for the moral law. Recall that here "respect" does not indicate a feeling received through influences, but rather as something self-wrought by a rational concept and, hence, a moral incentive for action. However, Heidegger goes as far as to claim that the original ground of this unity of reason and feeling is the transcendental power of imagination. For one thing, Heidegger regards transcendental imagination as mediating between practical reason and the feelings or desires of the person just as the way it mediates between sensibility and understanding. Then, he aims to interpret the rational feeling that is respect as a schema of transcendental practical imagination. In other words, as Llewelyn says, "the 'rational feeling' of respect earths the moral law in feelings" (Llewelyn, 2000: 7). Hence, respect, regarded as a schema, would then indicate the capacity to apply our moral concepts –for instance, duty– to our actions performed at a particular time.

As I have argued, the respect for law is the mediating factor between the moral law and the self. Besides, I have also pointed out that within Kant's account of morality, the question of how to determine oneself completely by the law remains unanswered, although he claims that objectively moral law and subjectively respect for the moral law determine the self as moral. However, how moral law objectively determines the will is an insoluble problem of human reason. In other words, the possibility and the motivation to act upon unconditioned commands reside in the possibility of freedom. However, Heidegger focuses and lays emphasis on the function of transcendental imagination as disclosing the finitude of human reason. This leads him to elaborate a more original, unobjective and unthematic manifestation of the meaning of law and of the acting self (Heidegger, 1997: 112). Heidegger aims to show that the motivation to determine oneself completely by the law requires the self-submissive respect. The possibility of receiving moral claims rests on the possibility of a pure moral receptivity. Although the moral law issues from the self-legislation of practical reason, a form of pure receptivity, i.e. self-submission to the law, must accompany this spontaneous operation of reason. In this respect, the subjection, i.e. the submission of the self, and the subjectivity, i.e. the activity of the self, are one and the same in the receptive spontaneity of respect. Hence, the possibility of moral self-consciousness (its activity) resides in the ontological possibility of moral receptivity (in its passivity). For one thing, moral receptivity that is defined in terms of the feeling of respect is a mode of self-disclosure within which the true being of the self is given. The capacity to act under unconditional commands depends on the finitude of human person.

Insofar as we are finite beings, we have the ability to receive the moral law in the form of an unconditional imperative. Our susceptibility to be motivated by sources other than respect for the law exhibits our finitude. Heidegger claims that conformity to law presupposes our finitude. Therefore, human finitude should be the locus of the relation between being-human and law. As Schalow interprets, Heidegger searches for the ways "to sharpen Kant's analyses by showing that they depend upon a preliminary description of the structures defining human finitude" which are supposed to constitute his prospect of the ontology of human existence (Schalow, 1986: 139). Hence, responding to the authority of law is only possible by responsibility. In order to give response to law, one must offer oneself and, in offering oneself, one should be first open to oneself. Insofar as we are disclosed to ourselves in and through our finitude, we can respond to the obligation of the moral law. Finitude turns out to be one of the necessary conditions to receive and to respond to the call of the imperative. When Heidegger claims for the possibility of pure sensible reason, he aims to point out this unity of activity and passivity as pure self-affection of time corresponding to the pure self-affection of respect. The original time as pure self-affection is the unity of spontaneity and receptivity. For, on the one hand, the moral self, in submitting itself to the law and, in being affected by the call of the moral law, is passive and receptive. On the other hand, the law which the moral self is affected is given not externally but by the legislation of this self-same subject. In this sense, it is spontaneous and active. Therefore the structure of the moral feeling displays itself as pure self-affection and as such it is in unity with the structure of original time. This is the reason why the moral law and the true being of the self are rooted in the power of imagination which displays the essential structure of respect. The structure of respect for the law discloses the structure of authentic being-its-self, i.e. self-responsibility. Then, what is at the ground of the possibility of practical reason is this self-responsibility which is both receptive (receiving what one already has been) and spontaneous (responding to one's own self) at the same time (Heidegger, 1997: 111). Thus, in *Being and Time*, this productive unity of imagination signifies the unity of past and future in the present moment of decision. In the context of *Being and Time*, Heidegger elaborates the original time as disclosing its structure in the call of conscience and in the self-responsibility of *Dasein*.

Time and History: Anticipatory Resoluteness

In *Being and Time*, section 74, Heidegger exposes the being of the entity called *Dasein* as historicalness (*Geschichtlichkeit*). Thus, *Dasein* has its history owing to its ability to face its own death as its ownmost and inevitable possibility. However, what is the occurrence (*Geschehen*) that determines existence as historical? Heidegger says that the answer has to be sought in the phenomenon of anticipatory resoluteness which is grounded in temporality. What does anticipatory resoluteness signify? Does it specify the choices and the decisions that must be taken in order for *Dasein* to be itself? Anticipatory resoluteness, in Heidegger's analysis, is a formal structure without content. Miguel de Beistegui discusses this issue as follows:

> In anticipatory resoluteness, Dasein is made present to its own being in such a way that it can take it over wholly and be free for it. This means, in other words, that Dasein understands itself as this being which is both projected against its own end and thrown into a world. Through anticipatory resoluteness, the "there" or the situation of Dasein is made transparent to Dasein. The existential choices and attitudes that would follow from such a resolution are not discussed: they do not belong in the existential analysis… If an ethics or a politics could indeed unfold from this fundamental existential constitution, Heidegger refuses to consider it. Dasein's resoluteness remains empty. (Beistegui, 1998: 15)[6]

---

6   Accordingly, Beistegui argues that this qualification of resoluteness as being empty prevents us to identify it with heroism and voluntarism. Thus, in this context, Haar asks the following: "what are being-towards-death and running ahead if not the *forms* of *Dasein*'s self-appropriation, forms eternally devoid of content?" He argues these two forms can be identified with resoluteness "because the latter will be the existential that

What is the relation between anticipatory resoluteness and temporality? *Dasein* is historical in its being because of the anticipatory resoluteness which enables its being-an-occurrence. However, this occurrence of the being of *Dasein* is altogether grounded through the originary ekstatic temporality which makes possible all the modes of being of *Dasein*. In this respect, we can say that temporality is the *ratio essendi* of resoluteness where resoluteness is *ratio cognoscendi* of temporality (Haar, 1993: 31–32). Arguably, the authentic phenomenon of anticipatory resoluteness reveals the constitution of temporality and, in this regard, it has this function of disclosing the originary temporality of its own ground. The phenomenon of history is manifested by *Dasein*'s anticipatory resoluteness. However, what enables *Dasein*'s being as historical is this originary temporality, that is, its always already being temporal. *Dasein*'s Being-free for its ownmost ability-to-be depends fundamentally on the originary temporal axis of Dasein's being. Dasein is free only in the sense of being-temporal. Freedom is then grounded in the *finitude* of Dasein. Thus, Heidegger claims that "*Temporality gets experienced in a phenomenally primordial way in Dasein's authentic Being-a-whole, in the phenomenon of anticipatory resoluteness*" (Heidegger, 1962: 351).

Resoluteness is the way in which Dasein comes back to itself, or back to its original site (its 'there', *Da*) by gathering itself from its dispersion in everydayness. As anticipation, resoluteness signifies the decision to take up one's existence as finitude. Anticipation discloses this decision as the uttermost possibility of existence through which *Dasein* is liberated (Heidegger, 1962: 350). However, this coming back to oneself, or this gathering of the self is not an inward movement leading to the peace of inner life by cutting oneself off from the world. Rather, it is a movement of disclosure where *Dasein* confronts its own facticity, that is, its being-in-the-world, and places itself within the situation authentically. Hence, Beistegui claims that "it is a movement of disclosure, of clearing, where Dasein authentically ek-sists its own essence", that is, where it "comes back to its own ecstatic yet finite essence" (Beistegui, 1998: 15). This coming back to one's essence and gathering oneself as a whole constitute the process of appropriation, of becoming-proper (authentic). Yet, this process always involves a paradox which is described by Beistegui as follows:

---

can equally be existentiell in the form of a decision". Furthermore, it is in this respect that "the two allow *Dasein* radically to take hold of its initial disclosedness, to capture its own light, to enter absolutely into possession of itself, of its 'freedom,' to learn to 'choose its own choice'" (Haar, 1993: 15). Thus, in contrast to Beistegui, Haar interprets this as an extreme voluntarism.

Such, then, is the paradox of appropriation, of becoming-proper (of what is inappropriately referred as "authenticity"): Dasein gives itself to itself, it gives itself what from the start its *own*, and yet what is its own is also its gift, its heritage, which, as resolute, it takes over. A more traditional way of putting it would be to say that Dasein is free for its own necessity, that its authentic freedom is revealed in its ability to take up and take over the necessity of its own condition. It should be of no surprise, then, that the word Heidegger uses to define such ability is the *philosophem* that traditionally (at least since German Idealism) serves to designate the unity of freedom and necessity, namely, "fate" (*Schicksal*). (Beistegui, 1998: 15–16)[7]

We recall this paradox of appropriation from the Kantian understanding of practical realization of our rational, yet finite, essence on the way of our moral existence. In the Kantian approach, the moral law reveals the necessity of the action, and the freedom is realized by the action done for the sake of this moral necessity. The moral law from the start belongs to the pure practical rationality. However, it is also the "gift" of reason which we must take over. This similarity between the Heideggerian and the Kantian structure of appropriation of what is one's *own* is already apparent in their understanding of the double structure of human existence, and is presupposed in their different ways of coming to terms with this doubleness. Nevertheless, they both try to come to terms with this doubleness in their attempts to sustain the unity of freedom and necessity, that is, in their proposed solutions to the antinomy of law. Hence, the Heideggerian *Dasein* and the Kantian moral person are the sites which resolve this antinomy respectively in their authentic or autonomous modes of existence, that is, in their formal constitution, though they revolve within this antinomy in their everyday dispersion and disconnectedness. Heidegger says that if *Dasein* "wants to come to itself, it must first *pull itself together* from the *dispersion* and *disconnectedness* of the very things that have 'come to pass'" (Heidegger, 1962: 441–2). With respect to its structure, this is quite similar to the Kantian understanding of the determination of will by *a priori* principles devoid of empirical content. The moral person should discard the effects of his empirical nature on the pure practical principles of action. Hence, formally, for both Heidegger and Kant, resoluteness (authentic or moral) is the loyalty of existence to its *own* self (Heidegger, 1962: 443). Hence, Michel Haar claims that, for Heidegger, resoluteness is the very search *for* the pure form of the self in one's ownmost temporality (Haar, 1993: 56). Its correlate

---

7   In *Being and Time*, Heidegger draws a distinction between fate (*Schicksal*) and destiny (*Geschick*). Fate is used for the historizing of a resolute individual whereas destiny is for the co-historizing of the community, of a people. There is destiny because fateful *Dasein* exists essentially in being-with-Others (Heidegger, 1962: 436).

in Kant is that resoluteness is the very search *of* the pure form of self in one's ownmost finite freedom. This difference indicates that resoluteness, for Kant, presupposes the pure form of self in its search, whereas it is, for Heidegger, the existential, searching the pure form of self as constituted by temporality. The freedom is presupposed in the Kantian understanding of resoluteness as something moral, whereas for Heidegger, it is constituted ontologically as temporal.

Moreover, for both Heidegger and Kant, the possibility of authentic (Heidegger) and autonomous (Kant) relation to the other is possible within the conditions of self-relation.[8] The possibility of this specific self-relation is neither mediated, nor determined by the self-relation of the other. The Heideggerian *Dasein* and the Kantian moral person become what they *are* with respect to their self-relation, that is, with respect to the call which in any way belongs to them as their ownmost possibility. Their submission to this call and their response to its appeal are regarded as the only possible ways of self-appropriation. Moreover, the authentic self-relation of *Dasein* is always already posited. It is not something to be constituted by the others, but rather something posited by the formal constitution of *Dasein* from the beginning. Therefore, the ethical dimension of Heidegger's thinking, in this context, remains formal. Then, the question is whether one can separate the questions concerning the formation of self from the questions concerning the formation of community, i.e., the personal from the political. Moreover, the problem is to think the relations between ethics, politics and metaphysics without ever presupposing and positing the condition of the possibility of their difference and identity. Both for early Heidegger and Kant, this triune relation depends on the formal constitution of the self. The community, the kingdom of ends, being-with-others are regarded as possible on the ground of this self-relation.

The self, in the final analysis, is appropriated through its own effort in order to be what it *is*. Unlike Kant, for Heidegger, this verbal sense of "*is*" is the whole issue, and it is nothing other than the historical existence of *Dasein*. The originary historical happening of *Dasein* is fate which signifies *Dasein*'s ability

---

8 Joanna Hodge claims that this relational conception of human being manifests the ethical dimension of Heidegger's thought. Thus, she says that "*Dasein* is a form of self-relation which is systematically connected to others of the same kind, others of different kinds, and to the ground of possibility of there being such difference and otherness at all: to being" (Hodge, 1995: 2). I agree with her description that *Dasein* is a form of self-relation, and argue that this self-relation in its authentic mode is not mediated by the self-relation of the other. Instead, this self-relation is the only possible ground (the presupposition) of the authentic being-with-others.

to be (*Seinkönnen*), i.e. its finite freedom. Heidegger states *Dasein*'s primordial historizing, namely, fate, as follows:

> Once one has grasped the finitude of one's existence, it snatches back from the endless multiplicity of possibilities which offer themselves as closest to one -those of comfortableness, shirking, and taking things lightly- and brings Dasein into the simplicity of its *fate (Schicksal)*. This is how we designate Dasein's primordial historizing, which lies in the authentic resoluteness and in which Dasein *hands* itself *down* to itself, free for death, in a possibility which it has inherited and yet has chosen. (Heidegger, 1962: 435)

What gives *Dasein* its goals and particular possibilities is its being-free for death (Heidegger, 1962: 435). Death is the uttermost necessity. Yet, being-free for death is to choose this necessity as one's ownmost possibility. This is to choose myself since "choosing-death-as-the-only-possibility-belonging-to-me" discloses my other existential possibilities, and discards the accidental and provisional ones. This inherited, yet chosen possibility displays the structure of history, of fate, and of temporality as the ground that unifies freedom and necessity, transcendence and facticity, projection and throwness. The possibility of finite freedom resides in the facticity of freedom. Freedom is always already bound by the possibilities that it unfolds. As Schalow claims, "freedom, insofar as it only becomes manifest within the expanse of our limitations, is essentially finite" (Schalow, 1992: 296). It is in this respect that freedom does not belong to the Kantian intelligible realm, and is not something exclusively intelligible. *Dasein*'s primordial temporality, as the unitary ground of freedom and necessity, of future and past, aims to dissolve the problem in the antinomy of law.

Freedom is the possibility of *taking over* one's own throwness, which is possible by *handing down* to oneself the possibility that one has inherited. Yet, this taking-over signifies a primordial projection into one's "can-be", into the realm of possibility, into the futural horizon. Freedom can take place in the horizon of future in the sense of anticipating one's ownmost possibility. However, what one takes over is always what one has already been, that is, an inherited, yet chosen (because it is taken over) possibility. This "having-been-ness" of *Dasein*, this inheritance, is not something left behind and completely past, but in so far as it is *repeated*, it temporalizes itself only from out of and in the future. In traditional terms, we can say that past necessity temporalizes itself in the futurity of freedom, and the futurity of freedom regains its future from the inheritance of this necessity. This is to say that neither necessity is absolutely necessary, that is, it carries possibilities to be taken over, nor possibility (or freedom) is in absolute terms possible since it always already hands down the necessity it has inherited. Finally, Heidegger carries the Kantian antinomy back into a perspective of ecstatic horizonal temporality, and shows that both freedom and necessity, not in their antinomical structure, but in their unity, rule in the simplicity of the fate of *Dasein*. In this respect, he tries to overcome the antinomical structure of freedom and necessity by exposing the belonging togetherness of being and time in the existence of *Dasein*.

In Heidegger's words,

> Only an entity which, in its Being, is essentially *futural* so that it is free for its death and can let itself be thrown back upon its factical "there" by shattering itself against death –that is to say, only an entity which, as futural, is equiprimordially in the process of *having-been*, can, by handing down to itself the possibility it has inherited, take over its own throwness and be *in the moment of vision* for 'its time'. Only authentic temporality which is at the same time finite, makes possible something like fate –that is to say, authentic historicality. (Heidegger, 1962: 437)

For Kant, antinomy is the key to the discovery of transcendental idealism. It is attempted to be solved by the transcendental distinction between *noumena* and *phenomena*. For Heidegger, although he did not explicitly refer to this antinomy, it is a pathway leading to the discovery of the fundamental ontology. As I interpret that this antinomy finally leads to his attempt to provide a unitary existential structure of *Dasein*'s being, its dissolution is regarded in recalling the ontological difference between being (*Sein*) and beings. Then, for both Kant and Heidegger, the antinomy would be the outcome of a failure, or a problem arising from the dogmatic metaphysical accounts and requiring dissolution by giving up these metaphysical assumptions responsible for the contradiction. In particular, for Heidegger, constituting an adequate response to the forgotten ontological difference which would indicate the source of antinomy is possible by a historical-destinal occurrence. The essential element of this occurrence is designated as repetition (*Wiederholen*), which is handing down explicitly the possibilities of *Dasein* that "has-been-there" (Heidegger, 1962: 437). [9]

Conclusion: From the Destiny of the Hero to the Destination of Being

In *Davos Lectures*, Heidegger states that "I did not give freedom to myself, although it is through Being-free that I can first be myself" (Heidegger, 1997: 181). *Dasein*'s ability to be (*Seinkönnen*) displays the freedom as the form of self-appropriation within its finite horizon, i.e. its ecstatic-temporal existence.

---

9   See for more discussion, (Beistegui, 1999: 283–291).

This destinal existence of *Dasein* is characterized with the expression "hero". Zimmerman describes the Heideggerian "hero" as follows:

> The hero recognizes that the key to human freedom lies in submission to internal neces-
> sity. To be free means to understand oneself by letting oneself become what one has
> been fated from all eternity. This is no arbitrary, free-floating freedom; nor is there a
> blind, mechanical compulsion which catches us in an exorable causal chain. The human
> self can be free only when it recognizes that what is most possible within the self is also
> what is still determinative for the self – fate. In choosing this internal necessity, the self
> decides for temporality and finitude. (Zimmerman, 1981: 152)

This is the way Heidegger searches for a perfect complementarity between necessity and freedom, not as the complementarity of two different types of causality,
but as the primal event of appropriation (*Ereignis*). This event happens as the
existential structure of *Dasein*, that is, as the individual ecstatic-temporal existence. Then, the relation between the meaning of law and being-human is conceived within the terms of this event of appropriation, i.e., the self-appropriation
of *Dasein*. Hence, the ground law would reside in nothing but in the self-
appropriation of *Dasein*, that is, in the simplicity of its fate that is grounded in
its self-responsibility.

Much later, in *Schelling's Treatise on the Essence of Human Freedom* (1936
summer semester lecture), Heidegger questions the place of freedom in the
whole of beings. Thus, Heidegger says that, in Kant, the question of freedom is
still formulated as the opposition of nature and freedom (Heidegger, 1985: 60).
For one thing, in Kant's understanding, freedom is still mastery over sensu-
ousness, and since freedom as autonomy is placed exclusively in man's pure
reason, it is separated from nature (Heidegger, 1985: 84). However, Heidegger
via Schelling points to a much more essential and profound conflict between
necessity and freedom, and regards philosophy – thinking – as the middle of this
original strife between necessity and freedom. Thus, he claims as follows:

> Philosophy can never be justified by taking over and reworking a realm of what is know-
> able,…but only by opening more primordially the essence of the *truth* of what is know-
> able and discoverable in general and giving a *new path* and a *new horizon* to the relation
> of beings in general. Philosophy arises, *when* it arises from a fundamental *law* of Being
> itself. (Heidegger, 1985: 58)

In his late thinking, Heidegger takes a turn (*Kehre*) from the project of fundamental ontology to the history of being (*Sein*). In this respect, the question of the
unity of freedom and necessity is no longer qualified as belonging to the unity
of temporal existence, but rather to the history of being unfolding as the strife
(*Streit*) between truth and untruth. This strife between truth and untruth is in

fact the strife between the phenomenal and the non-phenomenal. The middle ground of this strife is the *Da* (the "there") of *Dasein*. A certain configuration of man's belongingness to Being and Being's call of man constitutes the "there" (*Da*). The "there" is the concrete historical site that is held open by the event. In this respect, Heidegger transposes freedom into the register of the epochal truth (clearing, or *aletheuein*) of being. As Haar suggests:

> Man is only the "site" (*Stätte*) and the "occasion" (*Gelegenheit*), ... of a breakthrough of freedom which has its own realm. Man is free only to let freedom be ... It is the possibility that the totality of being should manifest itself. *It is the condition of possibility of any "metaphysical truth"*. (Haar, 1990: 3)

This is the reason why man is destined to being, to its letting-be (*Sein-lassen*) in order to be the open site (*Da*) of its manifestation. Man's belonging to freedom signifies man's being exposed (*ausgesetzt*) to unconcealment of being. This exposure, in return, constitutes man's being transposed (*versetzt*) into the open (Haar, 1990: 4). Man's being exposed and transposed into the open, its being-*there* (*Dasein*) is made possible by freedom, i.e. its breaking through as an epochal field. Hence, Haar states that the ontological emergence of man's freedom is dependent on the very emergence of that epochal field which man cannot alone decide (Haar, 1990: 5).

Then what is the status of human freedom, if it is conditioned by the epochal unfolding *of* being? What is the role of man's finite powers with regard to this excessive freedom of being? Does ontologizing freedom diminish human freedom? Does man owe his own freely creative powers –thinking, building, dwelling– to the freedom of Being? When Heidegger argues that freedom is not the property of human beings, he rejects the Kantian conception of freedom. Freedom is not the spontaneity of a cause, or the spontaneity of human will. As Wright claims, for Heidegger, there is human freedom only insofar as freedom "breaks forth (*durchbricht*) in the human being, taking possession of the human being (*ihn (den Menschen) auf sich nimmt*), thereby making the human being possible (*ihn (den Menschen) dadurch ermöglicht*)" (Wright, 1990: 19). Wright claims that Heidegger's ontologizing freedom consists in representing human freedom as the "effect" of the freedom of being (Wright, 1990: 20). This representation not only diminishes, but also paradoxically heightens human freedom by paving way to a hierarchy of those who are most destined by being. Being destines the ones who are most capable of instituting and embodying the truth of being, who are most able to be (*Sein-können*), that is, the creators who are the thinker, the poet, and the statesman (Wright, 1990: 20).

Given the fact that being destines man, this hierarchy seems inevitable since some *can* fulfill this destination and some *cannot*. Some can hear and follow the address of being and some cannot. Being-human is determined by the possibility of unfolding either as *Da-sein* (being-there, turning toward) or as *Weg-sein* (not being-there, turning away). This twofold unfolding assumes that man has no other choice than to be in two ways, that is, properly (appropriately) and improperly (inappropriately). Human freedom is then a modification of necessity, an "effect" of the need of being. By unfolding as *Da-sein*, human being participates in the freedom of being since she/he brings into *work* that which is assigned by being through her/his finite operation of gathering, instituting and grounding. For this reason, she/he cannot be regarded as the agent bringing an effect in this world, but only as the free region, or the open site, through which the advent of place, i.e., the "t/here", or the event of being, happens. The freedom of being happens only as the breaking forth of this free region, or of this open site, that is, as the breaking forth of what is possible in humanity, the possible-futural humanity. So being's letting-be (*Sein-lassen*), as the freedom that bursts open as the free region within which beings come into presence, is never exhausted with the finite operations of this free region (*Da-sein*) which is an operation displaying itself in the work of creators. For sure, creators who bring the being of beings into their work have some privileged status in the mysterious agenda of the event of being. However, the seemingly political question to recognize those who have these privileged statuses in the event of being is deep down left to the thinking of the history of being, that is, to the philosophical thinking as "it arises from a fundamental law of Being" (Heidegger, 1985: 58).

Above all, *Da-sein* is qualified as the futural possibility of man. It is the possibility that shows the mutual belonging of man and being (*Sein*). Heidegger understands being always in its verbal impersonal sense. Being is not a substance or an existence. In his late thinking, this verbal sense of being leads him to the notion of the event (*Ereignis*). Heidegger transforms the question of being-human into a question of how one finds oneself in this eventfulness of being. On the one hand, one finds oneself as turning toward being. This is the meaning of *Da-sein*. On the other hand, one finds oneself as turning away from being. This is the meaning of *Weg-sein*. Turning toward being consists in our fateful submission to the call and the question of being. Thus, being asks a place, a site for its unconcealment. Our humanity has to be this site of clearing by instituting the truth of being. Whereas, turning away from being consists in forgetting the question of being. It is to treat being as an answer, that is, as a substance, as a subject, as God, or as a being among beings. This is the concealment of being (*Sein*). Moreover, Heidegger claims that the twofold manner of being-human (our turning-away and turning-toward) is not at our disposal, but rather, at the disposal of being.

Heidegger regards freedom as belonging to the verbal sense of being. This verbal sense of being consists in letting-be, sending, presencing, destining, assigning, revealing, grounding and concealing, cloaking, withdrawing. There is the originary strife within this verbal sense of being. The strife between truth and untruth raises the question of being to which we as human beings should open ourselves. This strife should be maintained since it shows the truth of being. The strife within being is an imperative for us. It is conceived as our most primary and most original obligation.

In "Letter on Humanism", Heidegger says that man stands "ek-sistingly" in the destiny of being (Heidegger, 1978: 216). What Heidegger means is that the "*Da*-sein" of man consists in the disclosure of being. "*Da*", here, signifies nothing but the lighting as the truth of being itself. The destiny of lighting is the dispensation (*die Schickung*) of being (Heidegger, 1978: 216).[10] Furthermore, he claims that the assignment contained in this dispensation of being is law (*nomos*) (Heidegger, 1978: 238).

> Only so far as man, ek-sisting into the truth of Being, belongs to Being can there come from Being itself the assignment of those directions that must become law and rule for man. In Greek to assign is *nemein*. *Nomos* is not only law but more originally the assignment contained in the dispensation of Being. Only assignment is capable of dispatching man into Being. Only such dispatching is capable of supporting and obligating. Otherwise all law remains merely something fabricated by human reason. More essential than instituting rules is that man find the way to his abode in the truth of Being. (Heidegger, 1978: 238–239)

The ground of law (*nomos*) is the assignment contained in the dispensation of being. The dispensation of being is the destination of being without an assumed destiny. It is the way in which being gives (*es gibt*) itself to us as the abyssal grounding of law. Its grounding is abyssal because it happens in a mysterious and incomprehensible way. Above all, in Heidegger's thinking, being is both the being of beings, i.e., the truth that is instituted, disclosed and sheltered by beings, and always in excess of beings, i.e., the truth that conceals itself. In line with this, we face the double inscription of the "metaphysical" sense of law as instituted by

---

10 Heidegger, in *Early Greek Thinking*, characterizes the dispensation (*die Schickung*) of Being as *Moira*, fate (*das Schicksal*), as the "apportionment" which "is the dispensation of presencing, as the presencing of what is present, which is gathered in itself and therefore unfolds of itself" (Heidegger, 1984: 97).

man and the "pre-metaphysical" sense of law as the destiny and the assignment of being. The domain of the truth of being and, therefore, the ground of law must remain incomprehensible given that its grounding and unfolding cannot be only at our disposal. In addition, this domain is overpowering because it essentially unfolds in its counter-essence, that is, in its *un-truth* as the particularly instituted configurations of law. This domain is both the rule *of* mystery –mystery as the concealing of what is concealed– and the mystery *of* the rule as such which holds sway throughout our inevitable turning-toward or turning-away from this mystery (Heidegger, 1984: 132–133, 136). Given the incomprehensibility of the law of being, there arises the work of the thinker, the poet and the statesman as the inevitable erring and, as Heidegger says, "error is the space in which history unfolds" (Heidegger, 1984: 26).

The above conclusion shows us the limitation of Heidegger's thinking. Thus, Heidegger's thinking of being in its verbal impersonal sense as *Ereignis* is limited with an ethical indifference. The ethical and the political are subordinated to the impersonal critical judgment of the history of being. Can we interpret the ethical and the political relationship with the other person in terms of the "disclosure" of being? Can we interpret justice in terms of the "un-truth" of being? Does not Heidegger's thinking of being entail an obligation to the anonymous or the impersonal rule and power of the epochal understanding of being? Does not Heidegger's account subordinate the real origin of transcendence, i.e. the Good, to being?

Consequently, the problem that evolves around the question *how* the ground of law, in its own terms, determines, conditions, or destines being-human is not resolved but radicalized in the account of Heidegger. Thus the incomprehensibility of the origin of transcendence renders the meaning of being-human undecidable and tragic as always already on the way of erring. What I would like to point out is that if human responsibility consists in giving response to this irretrievable and incomprehensible origin of transcendence, then our response will become our norm that is always fallible in the face of history. Although the responsive openness to the mystery of being may configure as the norm for the poet and the thinker whose responsibility shall then consist in their response to the dispensation of being, it must not in itself become the norm for the statesman. Thus if it becomes the norm of the political, then any particular accomplishment in the political life can be justified as "erring" with an ethical indifference, that is, with reference to the way in which history unfolds. If responsibility in the life of the political consists in the response given to the rule of mystery, then the political will be deprived of its ethical significance no matter how it is instituted historically.

The "tribunal" of being in Heidegger is meant to be the "jurisdiction" of the realm of transcendence within which the ground of law must be comprehended in its incomprehensibility. This comprehension of the incomprehensibility of the ground of law is the condition of possibility of history in Heidegger. This jurisdiction, by being the ground of all norms, defines being-human as having no power to comprehend the ground of its judgement. In other words, we can never comprehend how this jurisdiction conditions, destines, determines and commands us. We can never comprehend the "how" of freedom, of history and of responsibility. However, we are obliged to follow the call of this jurisdiction by being free, historical and responsible.

Let me recall the ancient tragic vision of laws that is acknowledged in Antigone's cry: "They are alive, not just today or yesterday: they live forever, from the first time, and no one knows when they first saw the light" (Sophocles, 1984: 82). It sounds as an absolute obligation for "the unknown" and as a cry for the absence of destination that destines us. If we compare Antigone's words with the following quotations from Derrida's extended reading of Kafka's short parable *Before the Law*, we will see how Antigone's cry turns out to be a question that is still awaiting for a response in the life of the ethical and the political.

> We must remain ignorant of who or what or where the law is, we must not know who it is or what it is, where and how it presents itself, whence it comes whence it speaks. This is what *must* be before the *must* of the law (*Voila ce qu'il faut au il faut de la loi*). (Derrida, 1992: 204)
>
> The law is silent, and of it nothing is said to us. Nothing only its name, its common name and nothing else… We do not know what it is, who it is, where it is. Is it a thing, a person, a discourse, a voice, a document, or simply a nothing that incessantly defers access to itself, thus forbidding *itself* in order thereby to become something or someone? (Derrida, 1992: 208)

References

Beistegui, Miguel de (1998). *Heidegger and the Political: Dystopias*. London: Routledge.

Beistegui, Miguel de (1999). The Time of a Repetition. *Philosophy Today*. Vol. 43. No. 3. Fall 1999, pp. 283–291.

Çırakman, Elif (2001). *The Ground of Law and Being-Human: a Kantian Antinomy and its Repercussions in Heidegger and Levinas*. Unpublished Ph.D. Dissertation. Ankara: Middle East Technical University.

Derrida, Jacques (1992). Before the Law. In *Acts of Literature*, (Derek Attridge, Ed.). New York: Routledge.

Haar, Michel (1990). The Question of Human Freedom in the Later Heidegger. *The Southern Journal of Philosophy*. Vol. 28. No. S1. Spring 1990, pp. 1–16.

Haar, Michel (1993). *Heidegger and the Essence of Man*, (William McNeil, Trans.). Albany: SUNY Press.

Heidegger, Martin (1962). *Being and Time*. (J. Macquarrie & E. Robinson, Trans.). Oxford: Blackwell.

Heidegger, Martin (1978). Letter on Humanism. In *Basic Writings*. (D. F. Krell, ed. Trans.). London: Routledge & Kegan Paul.

Heidegger, Martin (1984). *Early Greek Thinking*. (D. Krell D. & F. Capuzzi, Trans.). San Francisco: Harper & Row.

Heidegger, Martin (1985). *Schelling's Treatise on the Essence of Human Freedom*. (Joan Stambaugh, Trans.). Athens: Ohio University Press.

Heidegger, Martin (1988). *The Basic Problems of Phenomenology*. (A. Hofstadter, Trans.). Bloomington: Indiana University Press.

Heidegger, Martin (1997). *Kant and the Problem of Metaphysics*. (Richard Taft, Trans., Fifth Edition). Bloomington: Indiana University Press.

Hodge, Joanna (1995). *Heidegger and Ethics*. London: Routledge.

Kant, Immanuel (1956). *Critique of Practical Reason*. (L. W. Beck, Trans.). New York: Liberal Arts Press.

Kant, Immanuel (1965). *Critique of Pure Reason*. (N. K. Smith, Trans.). New York: St Martin's Press.

Llewelyn, John (2000). *The HypoCritical Imagination*. London: Routledge.

Rose, Gillian (1984). *Dialectic of Nihilism*. Oxford: Basil Blackwell.

Schalow, Frank (1986). *Imagination and Existence*. Lanham: University Press of America.

Schalow, Frank (1992). *The Renewal of the Heidegger-Kant Dialogue*. New York: State University of New York Press.

Sophocles (1984). Antigone. In *The Three Theban Plays*. (R. Fagles, Trans.). London: Penguin Classics.

Wright, Kathleen (1990). Comments on Michel Haar's Paper, "The Question of Human Freedom in the Later Heidegger". *The Southern Journal of Philosophy*. Vol. 28. No. S1. Spring 1990, pp. 17–22.

Zimmerman, Michael E. (1981). *Eclipse of the Self: The Development of Heidegger's Concept of Authenticity*. Athens: Ohio University Press.

Emrah Konuralp

On Positivism and its Methodological Individualist Revision

The historical development of the social sciences is conspicuously marked by one theory of social science, namely positivism. In this chapter, in a departure from rival ontological and epistemological premises that composed the basis of positivism, the methodological individualist revision of this theory is elaborated. This chapter also discusses the very logic of positivism and its major methodological limits to the social enquiry that paved the ground for alternative research theories. The main argument here is that positivism emanated from the historical conditions following the French Revolution and together with methodological individualism, they have been in the service of sustaining or restoring 'order' rather than understanding or changing social reality.

Seeing the social world and the world of nature either as distinct realities or as in conformity with each other, composes "the primal problem of the philosophy of the social sciences" (Bhaskar, 1989: 66). Those arguing for the distinction of social and natural realities assert that while the method of the former aims at explaining, that of the latter focuses on understanding (Popper, 1961: 20; Schutz, 1972: 49). The very source of the primal problem is related to the answer given to the question on the nature of social reality: is it material or ideal? In other words, the existence of social life "as a set of material phenomena" or "as a set of ideas that human beings have about the world" (Johnson, Dandeker, & Ashworth, 1984: 13). Materialism and idealism as mutually exclusive positions, constitute the two poles of ontological discussions. At one pole of the ontological spectrum, where the focus is on the material aspect of social reality, human action is regarded as "behaviour taking place within constraining material conditions" since those external conditions –be it climate, natural resources, physical bodies, etc. or forms of social organisation, productive systems artefacts, etc.– determine the limits of human potentialities (Johnson et al., 1984: 13). At the opposite pole, the peculiarity of human action rests on the usage of complex systems of linguistic signs and cultural symbols, as indicators of intentions and meanings to be interpreted (Johnson et al., 1984: 14). Therefore, this ontological viewpoint rejects the consideration of human action as behaviour which is an adaptation to material conditions.

The second problem to be solved following the nature of social reality, is concerned with how to understand social reality: is it nominal or real? Since it is impossible to comprehend social reality with all of its particulars, the first solution, namely nominalism, suggests that the social realm is described or explained by using certain concepts and these are the names attributed to particular events or things in this realm (Johnson et al., 1984: 15–16). For example, when we talk about secularism, we use this concept to refer to a political principle requiring the separation of state and religion. This concept is based upon the particular experiences in the West and then generalised. As an alternative to nominalism, *realism* argues, "the significance of scientific concepts lies in their capacity to 'reveal' a social reality that is not immediately accessible to observation. Far from merely summarising observed particulars, such concepts actually penetrate to a reality that underlies and explains the particular events" (Johnson et al., 1984: 16).

Having the intention of producing empirically tested systematic secular knowledge on reality, the roots of social sciences as the facilitator of modernity date back to the sixteenth century. In this respect, the history of science indicates a process of liberation from forms of authorities like the church.[1] The classical scientific approach was based on two assumptions: the Newtonian model presuming symmetry between the past and the future, and the Cartesian dualism presuming distinctions between nature and humans, substance and reason, the material world and the social/immaterial world (Gulbenkian Commission, 1996: 2). Concomitant to these distinctions, when the empirical work came closer to the heart of scientific endeavour, division of knowledge into two 'separate but equal' domains as science and philosophy started to pave the ground for a hierarchical superiority of 'science'. By the nineteenth century, being separate and in opposition to other forms of knowledge, the term 'science' was equated with 'natural' (or 'positive') science (Gulbenkian Commission, 1996: 5; Popper, 1961: 2).

The French Revolution was accompanied by social turmoil, which intimidated the establishments in Europe into rationalising, organising and limiting the irresistible social and political change and into forming a new stable social order via the appropriation of the model of Newtonian physics to secure being 'positive'. For example, the need to extract accurate knowledge about social

---

1   Although the history of science is presented as a rivalry between divinity and secularity, it is a major concern that to what extend science can be liberated from 'secular' forms of authority like the state or the market.

reality forced some thinkers to speak of 'social physics'. "Science was proclaimed to be the discovery of objective reality, using a method that enabled us to go *outside* the mind, whereas philosophers were said merely to cogitate and write about their cogitations" (Gulbenkian Commission, 1996: 11). Another important development was the division of the inquiry of reality into separate disciplines. The disciplinarisation and professionalisation processes initiated the formation of new institutional structures "to produce new knowledge and to reproduce the producers of knowledge" (Gulbenkian Commission, 1996: 7).

The rival epistemological stances in investigating social realities fuelled those divisions. For example, while history got closer to art and literature in adopting an ideographic approach, which dwells on unique aspects of individual phenomenon, 'social science' was seen as nomothetic in looking to develop law-like generalisations on 'objective' social reality, just as in natural sciences.

Although the term 'positive' knowledge, based on natural phenomena was first used by Condorcet and Laplace, the pioneer of positivism[2] was Auguste Comte (1798–1857). This philosophical theory was an heir of the Enlightenment philosophy in a society where industrial developments had reached a head, and the prediction or direction of social upheavals could only be realised through systematic scientific knowledge. In this respect, coming to terms with social order and regularities became the ideological premise of positivism. For example, upon the destructive first phase of the French Revolution, Comte mentions the yearning to Progress and ascribes positivism to reconcile Order and Progress (Comte, 2000: 118, 2009: 63–76).

In Comte's understanding of 'positive' science, liberation from theology, metaphysics and speculation is of great importance: "Our researches, then, in every branch of knowledge, if they are to be positive, must be confined to the study of real facts without seeking to know their first causes or final purpose" (Comte, 1903: 21). In this way, positivists try to avoid ontological questions about the nature of reality and they leave such issues to philosophers.

For Comte (2009: 45), mathematics is the point of departure for reaching sociology as the intellectual synthesis. His hierarchical classification of sciences follows the order as follows: mathematics, astronomy, physics, chemistry,

---

2   Norman Barry (1995: xviii) refers to two usages of positivism: "First a positivist believes in the clear separation of fact and value and argues that theoretical and descriptive accounts of man and society can be made which do not involve evaluative judgements. (…) In the second and more extreme sense, it is the theory that only phenomena which are in principle capable of being observed are of any significance for social science." In this chapter, positivism is used in the second sense.

biology, sociology (Comte, 2009: 35). This classification led to further subdivision of social sciences. The ideological traces of such departmentalisation are clearly seen today (Bensussan & Labica, 2012: 768).

In fact, the order of disciplinarisation took place thus. Firstly, history became a distinct field of social sciences with the pressure on historians to write the history of their own nations. Relying on objective data derived from the archives, historians helped the demarcation and/or construction of 'nations' as newly sovereign peoples. Secondly, with the dominance of liberal economic theory, previously popular political economy left the field to 'economics', seeing economic behaviour in the market in terms of universal individualism. Thirdly, invented by Comte, 'sociology' became a distinct discipline to deal with social reform, discontent and disorder within society. Fourthly, 'political science' came to the fore by differentiating itself from political philosophy and dealing with the state and politics. The emergence of political science as a new discipline also helped justification of the separation of economics from political economy. Finally, with colonisation, the Europeans encountered other regions of the globe and they felt the need for ethnographically studying those indigenous peoples. Having an ideological aspiration, 'anthropology' emerged as a new discipline, distinct from the social sciences studying Western peoples.

In the process of the institutionalisation of social sciences, geography (the study of static spatial dimension was closer to the natural sciences), legal studies (laws did not emerge out of scientific investigation and it was impossible to make empirical research on highly normative context), and psychology (rather than being sprung from social sciences, phycology was considered within medical/natural sciences) remained outside the domain of social sciences (Gulbenkian Commission, 1996: 25–28). Once three nomothetic social sciences -economics, political science, and sociology- were distinguished from ideographic studies of history and anthropology, they emphasised their differences in terms of subject matter and methodology: "Economists did this by insisting on the validity of a ceteris paribus assumption in studying market operations. Political scientists did it by restricting their concerns to formal governmental structures. Sociologists did it by insisting on an emergent social terrain ignored by the economists and the political scientists" (Gulbenkian Commission, 1996: 31).

Following the Second World War, the lines of demarcation between disciplines started to be blurred. The end of colonialism and the emergence of newly independent states as the actors of history marked this development. Also, studies of regions as large geographic zones having "cultural, historic, and often linguistic coherence" summoned the three nomothetic social sciences, and history, anthropology and Orientalism in a multidisciplinary manner (Gulbenkian

Commission, 1996: 36–37). The basic political motivation for this was the need to transform the ex-colonies into markets via 'development' recipes of the modernisation school.

Rather than relying purely on positivist theory, a different set of social scientists from Marxian or Weberian perspectives argued for a more 'historicist' and less 'scientistic' explanation and description of large-scale social change (Gulbenkian Commission, 1996: 44). This line of analysis was called 'historical sociology'. These social scientists were critical of the ahistorical approach of positivist sociologists; of affiliation to order at the expense of analysing social change; and of application of Western concepts to the non-Western contexts. 'New economic history' in economics, 'new institutionalism' in political science 'historical anthropology' in anthropology, and 'historical geography' in geography were examples from other disciplines that were seeking cooperation with history (Gulbenkian Commission, 1996: 45). Asserting for cultural and historical relativity, the historicists argue that unlike laws of nature, complex social realities are time and space bound and meaningful within a particular historical situation (Popper, 1961: 5–6). Correspondingly, they reject positivist methodological presumption on using the 'scientific' method of 'positive' sciences. As Norman Blaikie (2007: 38) writes, "it is not possible to answer the question about whether the methods and procedures used in the natural sciences are appropriate in the social sciences with simple 'yes' or 'no'."

Whereas incorporating historical analysis to the social sciences raised methodological questions, the overlap of three nomothetic social sciences took place almost quietly:

> The sociologists led the way, making both 'political sociology' and 'economic sociology' into important and standard subfields within the discipline as early as the 1950's. The political scientists followed suit. They expanded their concerns beyond formal governmental institutions, redefining their subject matter to include all social processes that had political implications or intentions: the study of pressure groups, protest movements, community organisations. And when some critical social scientists revived the use of the term 'political economy', other, less critical political scientists responded by trying to give the term the subject matter a more classically nomothetic flavour. The common result, however, was to engage the political scientists in a fuller concern with economic processes. For the economists, the early post-war dominance of Keynesian ideas revived concern with 'macroeconomics', whereupon the dividing line with political science became less clear, since the object of analysis was largely the policies of governments and intergovernmental agencies. Later on, some non-Keynesian economists began to argue the merits of using neoclassical economic analytic models for the study of subjects traditionally considered sociological, such as the family or social deviance. (Gulbenkian Commission, 1996: 45–46)

These examples show that the lines of demarcation between disciplines are not absolute, but blurred. In this work, I argue that strict disciplinarisation as the ideological premise of positivism obscures the grasp of social reality. Instead, as the historical development of social sciences suggests, nonpermeable nomothetic social science disciplines were incapable of eliminating multidisciplinary quests. Another point is that the assertion of positivist nomothetic social sciences to reach universal consensus on measurable social phenomena was too much of an overstatement since the 'scientific' knowledge itself has evolved historically and the definition of universal truth has always changed as the loci of power switch.[3] Therefore, the disciplinarisation of social sciences is an ideological facet of the historically contingent universalism of positivism. Nonetheless, dividing social reality into spheres and social inquiry into demarcated disciplines are not 'natural' but ideologically constructed. As Colin Hay (2002: 68) notes, for example, in more restrictive specification of the 'political' and positivistic view of scientific method, there is a vested interest: "bound up in rigidly policing disciplinary boundaries and rhetorical authority conjured in the 'scientific' claims that positivism might sustain." Moreover, seeing politics in positivist terms as *arena* (or an institutional locus) means restriction of political analysis in the realms of the state or public sphere; however, when politics is considered as *process* of governing, political inquiry encompasses the uneven distribution of power, wealth and resources (Hay, 2002: 73). Therefore, for example, the strictly restricted 'disciplinary' boundaries between political science and economics are to be revised. As Hay (2002: 75) puts it, "the political is perhaps then best seen as an aspect or moment of the social, articulated with the other moments (such as the economic or the cultural)."

Concerning the debate on method of positive sciences and that of social sciences, according to positivists the scientific method of social inquiry has to be a reflection of the method of natural sciences in order to secure objectively observable knowledge about social phenomena. Being a quality considered with knowledge, theories, research methods, etc, objectivity embraces "the willingness to let our beliefs be determined by 'the facts' or by some impartial and nonarbitrary criteria rather than by our wishes as to how things ought to be. A specification of the precise nature of such involvement is a function of what it is said to be objective" (Longino, 1990: 62). Objectivity requires separation of 'facts' from 'values'

---

3   The significance of any historically contingent universalism is that "it provides the medium of translation while at the same time setting the terms of the intellectual discussion and is thus a source of intellectual power" (Gulbenkian Commission, 1996: 60).

and science has to be 'value-free' (Blaikie, 2007: 42). For Giddens (1974: 3) the requirement rests on "the idea that judgements of value have no empirical content of a sort which renders them accessible to any tests of their 'validity' in the light of experience." The positivist attack on the thinkers like Plato, Hobbes and Rousseau, the utilitarians who were concerned with values, was based on the criterion of meaning: that a proposition has to be analytically true by inspection or empirical verification; otherwise it is metaphysical, i.e. 'non-sense' (Barry, 1995: 4–5).

To secure objectivity, positivism asserts for a unity of method amongst natural and social sciences. Some positivists prefer the label of 'methodological monism' that "theories or hypotheses about social phenomena should be validated in ways that are not radically different from those used to validate theories or hypotheses about natural phenomena" (Blaug, 1992: 43). This doctrine means "that all theoretical or generalising sciences make use of the same method, whether they are natural sciences or social sciences" (Popper, 1961: 130). For Karl Popper (1961: 131), this very same method that can be called hypothetical-deductive method relies both on deductive explanations and testing them via predictions. Unity of science is, in an a way, reduction of all sciences to physics since scientific standards are universal (Benton, 1977: 12). This doctrine is called naturalism implying the application of logics of natural sciences to social inquiry because there is almost no difference between the behaviour of objects and human beings (Kolakowski, 1972; Popper, 1961; von Wright, 1971).[4]

In this line of analysis, the external reality composed of objects or events and the epistemological position varies accordingly: those objects or events are to be observed/experienced through senses or known by the use of reason. The former position is called empiricism and it is usually associated with naturalism while the latter is called rationalism having some sort of distance from positivism. Empiricism can be regarded as a strategy combing materialism and nominalism (Johnson et al., 1984: 19).[5] In the sixteenth and seventeenth centuries, experience and reason were asserted as two alternative foundations of knowledge which had been under the monopoly of revelation (Benton, 1977: 20). Therefore, empiricism and rationalism as competing theories of knowledge emerged from the challenge to religious faith. Benton (1977: 11) also notes that originally,

---

4   It is worth mentioning that with development of Einsteinian physics, the Newtonian paradigm on which naturalism rests is not a commonly shared position within natural sciences any more.

5   The concepts and generalisations in *nominal* terms are based on observations in the *material* world.

positivism is a variant of empiricism asserted by John Locke. If we compare the two epistemological stances, it can be argued: "while the empiricists, 'look at' the world in order to know it, on the grounds that what they can see or might see is all that exists, rationalists 'think' about the world in order to know it, on the grounds that behind the world that can be 'seen' or is given to the senses, there lies a world of thought; a structure that is innate, universal, and shared" (Johnson et al., 1984: 150–151).

Relatedly, another important point of distinction between empiricism and rationalism stands on the ontological separation of appearance and reality that only through reason and intuition can one "transcend the ephemeral world of surface appearance to reveal the structured reality beneath" (Hay, 2002: 77). Nonetheless, empiricists reject such a dichotomy since, for them, "the world presents itself to us in a direct, 'real' and unmediated way through our senses" (Hay, 2002: 78).

Apart from this distinction, in both positions, the reality is external to the individual since it exists independently of human beings. For example, "society is a *real* and *general* phenomenon; it is a thing-in-itself which stands 'outside' of, and is independent of, all those elements that make it up, such as individuals, their consciousness, and their circumstances" (Johnson et al., 1984: 149). "The scientist is thus viewed as a *subject* who is attempting to understand an *object* and is trying to be objective by eliminating bias that could lead to inaccuracy" (Doyal & Harris, 1986: 2). The external reality out there is assumed to be described or represented conceptually via language (Schwandt, 2000: 196). Once the social forms that humans created are treated as facts of nature or the result of divine will, we come across the fallacy of reification as we attribute reality to concepts or products of human activity and thus, the social world is objectified (Berger & Luckmann, 1967: 106).

In addition to this point, most of the objects of social sciences are abstract objects of theoretical construction used to explain certain experience (Popper, 1961: 135). However, it is a very common error in social inquiry "to mistake our theoretical models for concrete things" (Popper, 1961: 136). In this context, Karl Popper (1961: 28–29) compares and contrasts methodological essentialism designed to get inside the essences of things to explain them and methodological nominalism using words as instruments of description:

> Methodological essentialists are inclined to formulate scientific questions in such terms as 'what is matter?' or 'what is force?' or 'what is justice?' and they believe that a pene-trating answer to such questions, revealing the real or essential meaning of these terms and thereby the real or true nature of the essences denoted by them, is at least a neces-sary prerequisite of scientific research, if not its main task. Methodological nominalists,

as opposed to this, would put their problems in such terms as 'how does this piece of matter behave?' or 'how does it move in the presence of other bodies?'

In terms of positivism, using 'essences' as the ultimate explanation of reality is rejected (Yalman, 2010: 41). Similarly, Popper (1961: 136) criticises the explanation of changing observable events in terms of permanent essences presented by abstract models. However, for Popper (1961: 136), "the task of social theory is to construct and to analyse our sociological models carefully in descriptive or nominalist terms, that is to say, *in terms of individuals*, of their attitudes, expectations, relations, etc. - a postulate which may be called 'methodological individualism.'"[6]

There is no single universally accepted meaning of methodological individualism and this term incorporates ambiguities in its usage (Hodgson, 2007: 212). Methodological individualism in Popper's terms is a doctrine about explanation in social sciences. According to this doctrine, the explanation has to "be couched wholly and exclusively in terms of facts about individuals" (Lukes, 2006: 5). In other words, explanation in terms of collectives like states, nations, races, etc. is not found satisfactory (Popper, 1945: 91). For example, Hayek (1948: 6) writes: "There is no other way toward an understanding of social phenomena but through our understanding of individual actions directed toward other people and guided by their expected behaviour." In this respect, Popper's student Watkins (1957: 106) attaches importance to explaining social phenomena through deducing an account "from statements about the dispositions, beliefs, resources and inter-relations of individuals." Therefore, methodological individualism departs from a set of truisms which results in conflation of ontological individualism and methodological individualism:

> Society consists of people. Groups consist of people. Institutions consist of people plus rules and roles. Rules are followed (or alternatively not followed) by people and roles are filled by people. Also there are traditions, customs, ideologies, kinship systems, languages: there are ways people act, think and talk. At the risk of pomposity, these truisms may be said to constitute a theory (...) made up of banal propositions about the world that are analytically true, i.e., in virtue of the meaning of words. (Lukes, 1968: 120)

---

6 The debate on the primacy of system/society/structure over the actor/individual is crucial for the distinction between nominalism and realism: While realism focuses on 'social facts' or 'structures' of relations which are, sui generis and not reducible to their particular or individual elements, the point of departure of nominalism is the individual actor (Johnson et al., 1984: 17–18). Therefore, it is not surprising that Popper links methodological individualism to nominalism.

Regarding these truisms, a major point of differentiation between methodological individualism and positivist theory is about induction. As "induction moves from the particular to the general, from set of specific observations to the discovery of a pattern that represents some degree of order among all the given events" (Babbie, 2001: 34), the aim of reaching to law-like conclusions from empirical observations makes inductive thinking inevitable for positivist theory. For Barry (1995: 16), the positivist identification of science with the inductive bias is an unfortunate legacy that paved the ground to the liberal-rationalists who also claim to be 'positivists' by eliminating values from social sciences but at the same time rejecting the epistemological goal of positivism in coming to terms with empirical regularities of the social world: "Laws are not derived inductively but are *deduced* from a small number of simple propositions about human nature. The regularities revealed by social science are not historical or social 'facts' but our properties of human nature which can be assumed to be unchanging." For example, in the liberal theory of microeconomics, the price mechanism is explained with the generalisation of consumer behaviour that if the price of a good increases, the demand will decrease. This example is based on decreasing marginal utility theory that an individual will consume units of a good until the marginal utility of the last unit of the good equals its cost (Barry, 1995: 17).

Methodological individualism is applied not only to economic systems but also to the analysis of political systems:

> Social processes are understandable only as reconstruction out of individual actions. Collective words such as 'class', 'state' or 'society' do not describe observable entities, and statements containing them only have meaning when translated into statements about individual action. (...) The concept of man that underlies the methodological individualist's model based on a very few simple propositions about human nature: that men act so as to put themselves in a preferred position (though this does not have to be understood in purely monetary terms), that they prefer present to future satisfactions, and that they can have only a limited knowledge of the world around them. (Barry, 1995: 17–18)

Being 'a form of reduction', methodological individualism "claims that all social phenomena – whether process, structure, institution, or habitus - can be explained by the actions and properties of the participating individuals" (Elster, 1990: 47). However, the individual of methodological individualism is abstracted from historical context. For Adam Przeworski (1990: 64–65), due to the lack of historical and contextual information, the ontological assumption of methodological individualism on undifferentiated, unchanging, and unrelated 'individuals' cannot be defended. Similarly, Norman P. Barry (1995: 21–22) notes the weakness of liberal political theory:

> (…) that the account of the liberal self in individualistic rational-maximising terms seems to preclude these features of man which make social life possible. It is indeed true that much of liberal individualist social theory is under-pinned by a 'fragmented' view of the person: a view that works well enough in relation to explanation of the regularities of the market but is less satisfactory elsewhere. This fragmentation of the person involves the detachment of agents from their social settings and treats them as rational choosers or utility-maximisers.

Moreover, conflation of ontological individualism presupposes individuals as the ultimate constituents of the social world and methodological individualism precludes explanation of social phenomena with reference not only to individuals but also to their (social) relations. Positivists, on the other hand, would reject such an ontological commitment on the grounds of metaphysical assertion. They would argue for leaving such ontological debates to philosophers.

Another point of differentiation between methodological individualism and positivism stems from liberal-rationalist emphasis on rules and rule-following in explaining all social order, continuity and permanence (Barry, 1995: 18). Since the effects of rule-following cannot be tested empirically, positivists do not consider such an explanation 'scientific' (Barry, 1995: 18). Rather than rule-following, positivists like the founder of the behaviourist school Skinner (1972) argue that the 'learning process' results in conditioned behaviour of humans and this accounts for social regularities. Although positivism and methodological individualism differ in making an account of conformity and order, the adherence to *order* is in common. In other words, the widespread consensus on observing uniformities is the aim of social sciences "in spite of the differences of opinion with regards to the nature of explananda" (Yalman, 2010: 42).

As mentioned above, the most obvious characteristic of positivism is introducing ontological and epistemological questions as if they are *only* methodological threads, while methodological individualists merge ontological individualism with their methodological position to the extent considered by the positivists as falling into the trap of making a philosophical assumption. Despite this *minor* issue, positivism and methodological individualism go hand in hand. Hence, they are seen as 'strange bed-fellows' (Yalman, 2010: 40).

On the basis of the points mentioned above, as concluding remarks, it can be argued that positivism as a theory of social sciences is mainly a result of ontological contestation of materialism with idealism and epistemological contestation of nominalism with realism. It is shown in this chapter that positivism is a historically contingent theory, claims of which are assumed to be universal over a long period of time. The most obvious example to support this argument is about the conditions which emerged with the French Revolution, as the founder of positivism Comte felt the need to reconcile Progress with Order. In other words, the restricted disciplinary boundaries of nomothetic social sciences are not 'natural' but ideologically constructed. Also, seeing natural and social phenomena as identical or similar and asserting methodological monism between natural and social sciences, would result in ahistorical social analysis, which is apathetic to cultural and historical relativity. On the one hand, empiricism as a strategy combining materialism and nominalism serves to this positivist end of describing 'objectively' observed facts of the social world.

On the other hand, the ontological and epistemological assumptions that a researcher adopts are highly influenced by the researcher's ideological, educational and cultural background. Such an influence, therefore, determines the researcher's theoretical paradigm. In other words, the social embeddedness of the social scientist is to be acknowledged (Hay, 2002: 87). As Weber (1949: 72) puts it, "there is no absolutely 'objective' scientific analysis of (...) social phenomena." In this respect, value-free observation is questionable in a sense that observation is theory-laden, involves interpretation and therefore it is impossible to reach pure facts. It can be argued that "what are regarded as facts about social world are matter of intersubjective agreement, not detached, value-free producers" (Blaikie, 2007: 43). If the value-free objectivity of positivism is contestable, an alternative "version of objectivity that begins from values and is therefore situated within particular social contexts is possible" (Williams, 2005: 99). This kind of objectivity is "the purposeful search for truth about the properties of objects" (Williams, 2005: 110).

Concerning the methodological individualist derivative of positivist theory, it is shown that rather than rejecting it, Karl Popper made a revision of this theory by reasserting the strength of methodological individualism as a nominalist analysis of sociological models in terms of individuals. Yet it is a conflation of ontological individualism and methodological individualism, and this conflation means making an ontological assumption, which is unacceptable from positivist point of view. This conflation also forced Popperian methodological individualism to revise the inductive bias of positivism and replace it with deduction from a small number of simple propositions about human nature. One way or another, methodological individualism is a form of reduction with which the individual is abstracted from historical context.

It should also be noted that the general laws of social reality stem from regularities or constant conjunctions between events rather than causality since there is no causation in nature. In this context, causality is considered "as an *external* relation between two independently constituted entities" (Yalman, 2010: 41). "The task of scientific inquiry, therefore, would not enquire about the nature of social reality, but rather discover 'regularities' between 'contingently' related objects" (Yalman, 2010: 41). To put it in another way, the external world is composed of objects ('things') which would be considered as 'facts' by the use of senses (Giddens, 1972: 31). This means that positivism operates with the 'philosophy of external relations', "in which the boundaries between things are taken to be of the same order as their other sense-perceptible qualities hence determined and discoverable once and for all" (Ollman, 1993: 44). This "philosophy of external relations paved the ground for the original liberal assumption of the separation of politics and economics as if it is an appearing reality and (…) this taken for granted assumption overshadowed the specific social reality of capitalism depending on formal institutional separation of economic coercion from repression" (Konuralp, 2017: 9). In this respect, positivist disciplinarisation and liberal separation of economics and politics converge via the philosophy of external relations in order to fulfil the aforementioned ideological premise of positivism and liberalism.

References

Babbie, E. (2001). *The Practice of Social Research* (9th editio). Belmont: Wadsworth.

Barry, N. P. (1995). *An Introduction to Modern Political Theory* (3rd ed.). London: The Macmillan Press.

Bensussan, G., & Labica, G. (2012). *Marksizm Sözlüğü*. İstanbul: Yordam Kitap.

Benton, T. (1977). *Philosophical Foundations of the Three Sociologies*. London: Routledge & Kegan Paul.

Berger, P. L., & Luckmann, T. (1967). *The Social Construction of Reality*. London: Penguin Books.

Bhaskar, R. (1989). *Reclaiming Reality: A Critical Introduction to Contemporary Philosophy*. London: Verso.

Blaikie, N. (2007). *Approaches to Social Enquiry* (2nd ed.). Cambridge: Polity Press.

Blaug, M. (1992). *The Methodology of Economics or How Economists Explain*. Cambridge: Cambridge University Press.

Comte, A. (1903). *A Discourse on the Positive Spirit*. London: William Reeves.

Comte, A. (2000). *The Positive Philosophy Vol. II*. Kitchener: Batoche Books.

Comte, A. (2009). *A General View of Positivism*. New York: Cambridge University Press.

Doyal, L., & Harris, R. (1986). *Empiricism, Explanation and Rationality: An Introduction to the Philosophy of the Social Sciences*. London: Routledge & Kegan Paul.

Elster, J. (1990). Marxism and Methodological Individualism. In P. Birnbaum & J. Leca (Eds.), *Individualism: Theories and Methods*. Oxford: Clarendon Press.

Giddens, A. (1972). Introduction. In A. Giddens (Ed.), *Emile Durkheim: Selected Writings*. Cambridge: Cambridge University Press.

Giddens, A. (1974). *Positivism and Sociology*. London: Heinemann.

Gulbenkian Commission. (1996). *Open the Social Sciences*. Stanford: Stanford University Press.

Hay, C. (2002). *Political Analysis: A Critical Introduction*. London: Palgrave Macmillan.

Hayek, F. A. (1948). *Individualism and Economic Order*. Chicago: Chicago University Press.

Hodgson, G. M. (2007). Meanings of Methodological Individualism. *Journal of Economic Methodology, 14*(2), 211–237.

Johnson, T., Dandeker, C., & Ashworth, C. (1984). *The Structure of Social Theory: Dilemmas, Strategies and Projects*. London: Macmillan.

Kolakowski, L. (1972). *Positivist Philosophy: From Hume to the Vienna Circle*. Harmondsworth: Penguin.

Konuralp, E. (2017). Attempts on Non-Reductionist Marxist Theory of the State: A Stimulating Rehearsal or a Coherent Approach? *Cilicia Journal of Philosophy*, (3), 1–31.

Longino, H. (1990). *Science as Social Knowledge*. Princeton: Princeton University Press.

Lukes, S. (1968). Methodological Individualism Reconsidered. *The British Journal of Sociology, 19*(2), 119–129. Retrieved from http://www.jstor.org/stable/588689

Lukes, S. (2006). *Individualism*. Essex: ECPR Press.

Ollman, B. (1993). *Dialectical Investigations*. London: Routledge.

Popper, K. R. (1945). *The Open Society and Its Enemies, Volume II*. London: Routledge & Kegan Paul.

Popper, K. R. (1961). *The Poverty of Historicism*. London: Routledge & Kegan Paul.

Przeworski, A. (1990). Marxism and Rational Choice. In P. Birnbaum & J. Leca (Eds.), *Individualism: Theories and Methods* (pp. 62–92). Oxford: Clarendon Press.

Schutz, A. (1972). Concept and Theory Formation in the Social Sciences. In M. Natanson (Ed.), *Collected Papers I: The Problem of Social Reality* (pp. 48–66). The Netherlands: Springer.

Schwandt, T. A. (2000). Three epistemological stances for qualitative inquiry: interpretivism, hermeneutics, and social constructionism. In N. K. Denzin & Y. S. Lincoln (Eds.), *Handbook of qualitative research* (2nd Editio, pp. 189–213). California: Sage Publications.

Skinner, B. F. (1972). *Beyond Freedom and Dignity*. London: Cape.

von Wright, G. H. (1971). *Explanation and Understanding*. London: Routledge & Kegan Paul.

Watkins, J. W. N. (1957). Historical Explanation in the Social Sciences. *The British Journal for the Philosophy of Science*, 8(30), 104–117.

Weber, M. (1949). Objectivity in Social Sciences. In E. A. Shils & H. A. Finch (Eds.), *Max Weber on the Methodology of the Social Sciences* (pp. 72–112). New York: Free Press.

Williams, M. (2005). Situated Objectivity. *Journal for the Theory of Social Behaviour*, 35(1), 99–120.

Yalman, G. (2010). *Transition to Neoliberalism: the Case of Turkey In the 1980s*. İstanbul: İstanbul Bilgi University Press.

Eray Yağanak

Justice and Autonomy as a Solution for Public and Private Sphere Distinction

Liberalism is the most important turning point for the institutionalization of public and private sphere distinction. One of the most important contributions of this historical period was emphasis on the natural rights that individuals have autonomy, equality and justice. According to Liberalism, in general, "it is a fundamental moral truth that human beings may make valid and weighty claims in justice against each other, society and government. Human beings possess the moral rights in virtue of which they may make these claims of justice not as member of any specific moral community or as subjects of any positive legal order, but simply in virtue of their nature as the sort of creatures they are" (Gray, 2003: 45). The concept of justice has been the main axis of the discussions on the four concepts that I mentioned, and it has been thought that determining what is fair can also end the discussion on the other three concepts to a certain point. However, the debates over the concept of justice has laid the groundwork for the emergence of different theoretical approaches due to the lack of a implicit definitional basis for the concept, and the diversity of areas in which the concept is related. Numerous definitions stem from the fact that this concept is one of the main problems of the network of political, legal, economic, moral, religious relations that cover every aspect of social life The complex composition of this network of relations manifest itself in the relations of individuals[1]/persons with each other and themselves, in the relations between small communities, and in state/citizen, and the civil society/state relations. In this sense, as a consequence of this different network of relations, the problem of defining the concept of justice in different contexts arises. In this chapter, this problem will be examined as a problem of the network of relations expressed in the third relationship and in the context of the distinction between public and private spheres, which will be claimed to be an artificial distinction that damages the autonomy principle, disrupts the integrity of humanitarian action, creates different spheres of reality depending on the field of action. However, primarily, it will be discussed how

---

1 In this chapter, the notion of individual has been used both as a member of a group and as a citizen of a state. The meaning of the concept may vary according to the context of the sentence.

the network of relations expressed in the first two articles should be considered in a context different from the third article, and then the network of relations expressed in the third article will be examined in the context of public/private distinction.

The concept of justice can be evaluated in the scope of individuals or persons being "fair" to each other or treating each other in a fair way, when it is discussed in the framework of the relationship expressed in the first article, in the context of individuals/persons. Fairness, in this relationship, is considered within the framework of the concepts of "right" or "good," and for this reason, the action itself is valued in terms of the meaning attributed to the right and good concepts that the individual/person possesses. In other words, "value judgments" that a person or an individual attribute to daily relationships gain value. However, the fact that any person's value judgment or understanding and interpretation of a value is implicit to himself/herself, is a hindrance to take that evaluation as an objective reference point. This may be the expression of the uniqueness of that person, but this difference cannot be generalized. Therefore, the attitude of a single individual to a singular event or situation does not generally lead to a general conclusion about what should be "right" or "good" in relation to similar events or situations. Because similar situations may not necessarily require similar solutions. This brings with it the conclusion that practical problems cannot always be solved through general principles or that these principles cannot be used as a solution. The attitude of a particular person with respect to a particular situation may be in contradiction with the principle of universality that determines the attitude that should be taken in that particular case and that transcends the individual. In other words, the principle may not coincide with the individual practice. For example, the ethical principle of telling the truth may not be tackled separately from the existing situation in all circumstances. In a certain situation, lying can be preferred to telling the truth due to its consequences. For example, it may be necessary to lie to save someone who is about to be killed. Because, saving a person's life by lying is more valuable than the negative moral influence of lying on this person. However, in any case, someone who believes that it is necessary to tell the truth independently from the conditions and outcomes can behave differently. Therefore, people may exhibit different attitudes in the context of the event/phenomenon. But here, I would like to state that I am not advocating an ethical relativity when expressing that a single person's attitude towards a singular event/situation may not apply to other people and situations. Undoubtedly, every event/situation, even though it is similar to other events and situations, is subject to an evaluation process based on the conditions, individual's and the community's system of moral values. This is not a relativity argument, but rather a preference of one of the ethical or moral systems.[2] I want to emphasize here that the principles are transformable, despite their generality. This transformation, as mentioned above, manifests itself in a decision/judgment, which a person gives in a certain situation. More precisely, the general principles governing the direction of a singular action can be adapted to the intention of the person realizing the action and to the purpose of the action, the act or the facts. This case, contrary to popular belief, does not lead to deterioration in the general principle. The principle maintains its existence in accordance with the general acceptance and keeps the action under its influence at any moment. Hence, if the assumption that humanitarian actions are carried out on "intention" and "aim" is accepted, it will become clearer that I want to emphasize that these intentions and aims are changeable.

A similar situation applies to small communities. Principles and value judgments, which constitute the inner working and structure of a community, and which are formed within relations of communities in themselves and with each other, are binding for all the members of the community. These rules and value judgments exhibit a closed, homogeneous property, and they are not possible to be generalized. For example, the principles and values that regulate the relations of members of a group that prefer a homosexual relationship to a heterosexual relationship, and the whole sense of meaning given to these principles may be different from the frame of meaning of principles of a group that prefer a heterosexual relationship. In other words, being right or wrong can manifest itself as an inherent trait to the community itself. A behavioral pattern that is right or good for a group may or may not be right for another or it may be considered bad. It can be said that a similar situation may apply to communities with a different cultural belief/faith. For example, the lifestyle that applies to the Amish and the principles governing this lifestyle, like religious rituals and non allowed extra community marriages, are innate to the community and exhibit a self-enclosed property. Therefore, the general principle here can also be interpreted differently for different communities and can be adapted to the

---

2   Two different ethical theories about the consequences of actions or actions that need to be taken into account, regardless of consequences, are (*Utilitarianism*) and (*Deontology*). While utilitarianism emphasizes that what is morally right is the benefit of action as a result duty ethics concentrates on a general principle, from which actions derive themselves, regardless of their consequences. For more information on these two perspectives, see: Bentham, Jeremy, Mill, John Stuart (2004) "*Utilitarianism and Other Essays*", ed. Alan Ryan, Penguin: UK, Kant, Immanuel, (1991) *The Metaphysics of Morals*, trans. Mary Gregor, Cambridge University Press: New York.

community. However, being self-enclosed does not mean being unrelated with others, and fictionalizing the relation with others over differences. On the contrary, it means that the different lifestyles that appear depending the conceptual framework of reality the relationship is fictionalized through are required to be "recognized"[3] in order to sustain their existence. This recognition goes beyond the normative doctrines that advise and insist that the intrinsic behavior patterns of the first two networks of relationships that I mentioned should be in accordance with the general principles. Because normative claims can lead to disregard of the "difference" principle, which is intrinsic to liberal democracy. Such a situation may result in imposing artificial boundaries between private and public sphere, with the idea of "privacy", the distinguishing feature of the principle of autonomy. What I mean here is that instead of maintaining a normative attitude which suppress different ways of life that individuals have, we should consider a kind of "value pluralism" proposed by Joseph Raz. According to Raz,

> Value pluralism is intimately associated with autonomy. [...] It is that autonomy is valuable only if one steers a course for one's life through significant choices among diverse and valuable options. The underlying idea is that autonomous people had a variety of incompatible opportunities available to them which would have enabled them to develop their lives in different directions. Their lives are what they are because of the choices made in situations where they were free to go various different ways. The emphasis here is on the range of options available to the agent. This points to a connection between autonomy and pluralism. A pluralistic society, we may say, not only recognizes the existence of a multiplicity of values but also makes their pursuit a real option available to its members (Raz, 1995: 119–120).

Value pluralism seems to presuppose the existence of the rights people have. In this sense, in the first two relationship networks I have mentioned above, the condition of actions to gain value both singularly and holistically is connected to the idea of rights of these actions. In this sense, one of the concepts that should be taken into consideration in the discussions on the concept of justice is the notion of "rights". Although the notion of rights can be discussed in many ways (political, religious, economic, gender, etc.) just like the concept of justice, this concept is generally examined in terms of ethics and law. Thus, although the definitions of rights for these two domains do not entirely exclude each other, they at least differ descriptively. One of the most important reasons why the definitions differ is the distinction between "Private sphere" and "Public sphere".

---

3 For a detailed discussion on the concept of recognition, also see. Taylor, Charles (1994) "*Multiculturalism*", Expanded edition, ed. Amy Gutmann, Princeton University Press: United States.

Because this distinction also reveals a discussion of on which fields the right is supposed to be used. This debate is carried out in a framework that includes both the duties and obligations of the two parties to each other in citizen-state relationship. The most important problem here is the conflict between duties and obligations. In other words, having a right also requires the fulfillment of duties and obligations inherent to that right. However, duties and obligations require the right that is assumed to be fulfilled to be explained or determined regarding what kind of right it is. In this sense, it is appropriate to mention two kinds of rights here. In fact, the rights that are supposed to be possessed in terms of being human can also be evaluated in the context of these two rights. For example, the right to live, expressed as one of the most basic rights, is not a right possessed merely for being a human being. This right has a direct relation with legal and ethical (moral) rights that will be mentioned. I will try to explain what I want to say with an example. Let's suppose that any person has the right to continue his/her life in terms of being only human (I exclude the argument of what is being a human). This is both a legal, if that person is a member of a state and bound to the laws of that state, and a moral right. But, let's suppose that the same person wants to end his/her life. In principle, disconnected from the legal context, that person is entitled to this right and may use his/her right when appropriate circumstances arise. In other words, the general principle that existence should be maintained under all conditions may not be valid here. However, in legal sense, the right to commit suicide may not be legally recognized. In such a case, can it be considered that he/she has failed to fulfill his/her duties and obligations to him/herself and the social/political structure which this person is a member of? Therefore, it seems necessary to make a distinction between these two rights. The rights I try to express are legal and moral rights. Undoubtedly, it is necessary to discuss what should be understood from the concept of "right", first. But I will not elaborately refer to this discussion. I will continue my discussion only in the context of legal and moral rights. My intention here is to make it clear that the private/public distinction is artificial in debates about which action can be carried out in which field.

Above, I have argued that the most basic right that a person has in nature, in terms of being human, is not just the right to life since the fact that the right to life requires the existence of sustainable conditions and social/political space. The right to life cannot be mentioned in an environment where these do not exist, because a right is only granted when it is approved by others. But let's look at what should be understood from natural right, which is also the source of right to life. The natural right that every single human is supposed to possess, as Hobbes claimed, "The Right of Nature, which Writers commonly call

Jus Naturale, is the Liberty each man has, to use his own power, as he will himself, for the preservation of his own Nature; that is to say, of his own Life; and consequently, of doing anything, which in his own Judgment, and Reason, he shall conceive to be the aptest means thereunto" (Hobbes, 1996: 91). This definition is certainly not the only answer to the question of what "natural rights" are. Nevertheless, based on this definition, taking into account the above-mentioned claim, let us try to analyze what is meant by the right to life, which is called the most basic right. But remember that this definition is a definition related to a pre-communal natural state. In fact, this definition does not require a detailed analysis. With a sentence and a few questions, we can explain this definition. "Do whatever you want to do." For what? "To survive." What about the rights, law, and respect to others' life and property? They have no meaning. But is it really like that? Is such a life possible? Undoubtedly, the condition of being called a human requires being a part of the same kind of beings and being among them. If such a situation does not exist, it does not make any sense to speak of law and rights. For every general principle, we can then link the condition that every general principle is applicable to the fact that that principle is primarily a product of the human mind and is accepted de facto by the majority of the people that constitute a society. We can say that, the debate about the moral and legal boundaries of humanitarian action arises from this acceptance. As I mentioned above, what I mean by saying that the most fundamental right that a person has as a human being is not the right to live gains meaning here. If a person is not among his/her own kinds and if his/her existence is not confirmed by other people, the right to live does not appear in that person. There is no doubt that he/she wants to continue his/her life. But he/she cannot see that as a right and he/she acts only with the instinct to survive. That puts him/her in the position of an ordinary living being. In such a case, a discussion of justice cannot even arise. Then, the condition of concepts of public/private sphere, justice, rights and autonomy to acquire content depends on the relation of these conditions with the society. I said there was no point in talking about these concepts for a person who does not live with the beings from his/her own kind. Now, let's continue our discussion with the fact that we are living beings in a society. Consequently, let's continue to discuss the relationship between these concepts in the light of the following questions and try to clarify the relations between the concepts of justice, rights, public/private sphere and autonomy. What is public sphere? What is private sphere? What do we mean by public and private?

The public sphere is "a domain of our social life where such a thing as public opinion can be formed where citizens deal with matters of general interest without being subject to coercion to express and publicize their views" (Habermas,

1997: 105). In this sense, the public sphere is a place of affirmation and negation, in which private and personal thoughts and feelings are shared. Affirmation
corresponds to continuity even though it may have potential contradictions in
itself, and negation is a situation in which thoughts and feelings are interrupted.
This process of affirmation and negation leads to a debate between public and
private, both politically and ethically. In the broadest sense, the discussion
focuses on the necessity of making a distinction between the public and the private. In this sense, one side of the debate is related to the use of the rights gained
in terms of being a member of the state, while the other is related to the contradiction between the use of natural rights, which are assumed to be possessed
in terms of being human. In fact, the main problem is related to the tension
between the ruler and the ruled from another perspective. However, the relationship between the ruler and the ruled that have been mentioned here is not
a tension in the sense of Plato or Aristotle, about who will be the ruler and who
will be the ruled. This is a secondary problem. The main problem in this regard
is about the participation in public affairs in general terms, and, in particular,
about the protecting or maintaining the interests and benefits of this participation. In other words, active involvement in decision-making processes in the
public sphere is also related to personal interests and benefits, and, in a broader
sense, sustaining private life despite the public. Of course, we cannot expect
every single person's interests, wishes and benefits to be met in public sphere.
Such a demand means preferring a chaotic environment to order. In this sense,
even though the differences between people are tried to be solved by the idea of
equality before the rights and the law, this ideal cannot be realized. The reason is
not only that this is a legal and political problem but also an ethical problem and
that the boundaries between the public and the private cannot be easily drawn.
Nevertheless, at least to start from an appropriate point, it will be useful to provide a general framework to show how the meanings of those terms are protean.
According to Weintraub, four frameworks are to be considered when we try to
clarify what role they play in relation to our connection with each other and
state, namely in our social, political, ethical and economic lives. These are;

1. The liberal-economistic model, dominant in most "public policy" analysis and in a
great deal of everyday legal and political debate, which sees the public/private distinction primarily in terms of the distinction between state administration and the market
economy. 2. The republican-virtue (and classical) approach, which sees the "public"
realm in terms of political community and citizenship, analytically distinct from *both*
the market and the administrative state. 3. The approach sees the "public" realm as a
sphere of fluid and polymorphous sociability, and seeks to analyze the cultural and dra-
matic conventions that make it possible. 4.A tendency, which has become important

in many branches of feminist analysis, to conceive of the distinction between "private" and "public" in terms of the distinction between the family and the larger economic and political order -with the market economy often becoming the paradigmatic "public" realm (Weintraub, 1997: 7).

These four frameworks that Weintraub has drawn to show the depth of meaning that are intrinsic to the concepts of public and private spheres are important to see the extent of the debate on these concepts. The fact that humanitarian actions are determined according to different social, political, economic, moral, legal relations requires both the nature of human actions and the conditions affecting this nature. In fact, what is essential is the creation of conditions that do not interrupt the primacy of autonomy. Such a condition is that the social, political, economic, moral and legal institutions that I have expressed are formed by taking into consideration the principle of equality. When these conditions are established, the negations caused by the understanding of formal justice can be removed and justice can be made to appear in the context of events and facts. However, the uncertainty of the nature of humanitarian action may prevent this from happening. In this sense, it would be appropriate to talk about the nature of humanitarian actions.

Human beings perform their actions under rational and emotional influences. However, evaluations of how rational and emotional actions based on rational/ emotional decisions, which we can call the basis of humanitarian existence, are not adequate to determine the basis and the sphere of influence of this action. This inadequacy leads to the blurring of the public / private distinction that we can call the spheres of influence of this action, which makes the distinction of public/private space dependent on the nature of the individuals constituting the society. Consequently, it is impossible to draw the conceptual boundaries between the public and private spheres. This applies not only to those who evaluate an action but also to the person who carries out the action. For example, a person may not approve a political formation, that he/she politically supports in terms of public policy, because of his/her ethical perception. In this sense, this person may ignore his/her particular interests and benefits for the benefit of the public or the general, or the state or government may ignore the interests and benefits of that person in the name of the public interest. In other words, the parallel relationship that exists necessarily between both the demand and the pursuit of interests as a person and as a member of a state can turn into an asymmetric structure. Here I am talking about a process that can bring about an abandonment of interests and benefits in the public sphere, that can evolve to an acceptance of a priority/unimportance between the public and the personal, or the immanent lifestyle of two separate spheres. This can be handled by Aristotle's views in a framework close to the expressed meaning. When making distinction between the household (*oikos*) and the polis, Aristotle reduced this distinction to the imperatives that framed both areas and made the political and ethical boundaries between these two areas dependent on the area where the action was to take place. However, this did not mean that these two fields were independent of each other; because for Aristotle there was an organic connection between the continuity of the state and the welfare of the people. This connection corresponded to a continuity, in which both structures prevailed in relation to their inherent nature and ideal. This priority /unimportance relationship appeared to be a phenomenon that opened up a person's status of existence and the network of relationships, both in singular sense and in the sense of being a member of a community or a state. Historically, the explanations expressed in harmony or in parallel with the description of the nature and the process of existence in terms of both a single person and a society or the state in a pluralistic sense, actually assume this priority relationship. In this sense, a person gains meaning as a member of a state or society, or is excluded from the possibilities offered by society or the state in terms of rights. This makes the asymmetric relation mentioned above appear in the citizen/state relation. For example, according to Aristotle, as Shields claimed, "a stateless person is barely - or not at all- human. Minimally, human beings need the state to become fully actualized humans. Thus, the state needs no justification: its function is to permit humans to realize their ends" (Shields, 2007: 351). In other words "the state has a natural priority over the household and over any individual among us" (Aristotle, 1992: 60).

The distinction Aristotle made between the *oikos* and the *polis*, in other words, the distinction between the spheres in which the obligations and liberties prevail, and the priority of the *polis* over the people, is important for the understanding of the relationship between the whole and the part that constitutes it. This relationship, first of all, exposes the nature of the relationship between the state and the individual or citizen and, in a sense, provides an assessment of the statutes of public and private sphere distinction. In this context, although not all at the same level, theories that emphasize the priority of the state or the public historically and politically share a common root: the whole comes before the parts. Bobbio describes this situation as follows;

> We are dealing with an Aristotelian idea according to which the totality has ends which cannot be reduced to the sum of the aims of the individual members that compose it, and that, once the good of the totality has been achieved, transforms itself into the good of its parts; or to put it another way, the greatest good of the subjects is the effect not of its pursuit through personal effort and the antagonism of everyone's interests, but of

the contribution which each individual together with the rest can collectively give to the common good according to the rules which the whole community, or the group which directs it (apparently or in reality), imposes through its organs, be they autocratic or democratic (Bobbio, 1989: 14).

This priority relationship Aristotle established between the *polis* and *oikos* is inherently separated from theories of modern liberal politics, which assert the assumption that people naturally have a number of rights. In particular, social contract theories limit the use of these rights in the assessments of the rights the people naturally possess and their post-contract status by the laws of the state which they are a member of. In other words, the transfer of natural rights via contracts draws the boundaries for the use of these rights in the public and private spheres. Immanuel Kant, for example, who is involved in the liberal tradition, constructs the distinction between private and public spheres through individual happiness and the benefit of the public (state/society). The distinction between these two spheres is quite obvious. According to Kant, happiness related to personal or private is not included in the boundaries of the public sphere, and is not included in the regulatory principles of public administration. Because, according to him, personal happiness is all about the person's self and it is outside the legal applications that regulate social construction. In other words, according to Kant, the aim of the state is not to make people happy in accordance with their wishes, but to guarantee to sustain their happiness (Kant, 1991: 79). Thomas Hobbes, who is also a liberal, treats happiness, in other words, the peace environment in which there is no fear, as the basic desire of man, and as a means of escaping from any kind of conflict (Hobbes, 1991: 62–69), while Kant considers happiness as a goal. According to Kant, this is goal is not a desire, on the contrary, it is a necessity defined by the moral law of human actions (Rosen, 1993: 67). However, the determination of happiness as a necessary goal of man is not a sufficient reason to be happy. In order to sustain happiness, the conditions in which the individual / person is must also allow this. Kant's attitude at this point is quite clear. Kant associates this possibility with the protectorate of laws and defines happiness as a right. According to Kant, in a society and in a political structure, every person struggles to be happy, and decides what makes him/her happy by him/herself (Kant, 1991: 64). However, this decision process may nevertheless leave the person, as an autonomous entity, confronted with the obligation to choose. What I want to emphasize here is that; as an autonomous entity, freedom of action is protected by laws, and while autonomy is the basis of voluntary action, every action cannot be realized in everywhere as desired. In other words, the protection of the law may not be the guarantor of the action. In this sense, the right to choose a lifestyle other than the general one that was mentioned above and the will to choose this lifestyle, that is, the rights provided by being a person, and the rights provided by being an individual may be in conflict. To put it more explicitly, although the rights that arise from being an individual in the public sphere, or the rights that must be provided to the individual by the political authority, in general terms, encompass the rights provided by being a person, but these rights may not turn into action. In this sense, the autonomy in modern liberalism, the claim that personal interests and benefits should be protected in accordance with rational principles is important for understanding how the priority of the public to personal sphere should be understood. In liberalism, the priority given by the ancient Greek to public was reversed and the private sphere became the backbone of all ethical values. This situation reversed the idea that the part should be sacrificed for the whole, or should be contained within it. In other words, autonomy has become the basis of saving people from sacrificing themselves for the whole. The problem breaks out exactly here. How will someone who positions him/herself apart from the whole will continue to exist despite the general or the whole? Aristotle tried to solve this problem depending on the distinction he made between the *oikos* and *polis*. But now, these distinctions are not easily drawn, and boundaries cannot be determined. One reason for this is that, at least in terms of moral and legal boundaries, the value of an action depends on the person who performs this action. In other words, the value of life depends on the effect of the action.

One of the most important consequences of the idea of basing the value of life on the effect of action is that, it causes the idea that an act carried out in the "household" does not concern the public. One of the most important consequences of this cause is "indifference" and "loss of meaning" towards other lives. However, there is no meaning for an action that is not open to the other. In other words, meaning is relational. This relationship is also the basic foundation of being able to act as an autonomous entity. In this sense, the life that interrupts the thought of autonomy and that was imprisoned to *oikos* by the privacy means that, as Arendt claimed, "a state of being deprived of something, and even of the highest and most human of man's capacities." In other words, "a man who lived only a private life, who like the slave was not permitted to enter the public realm, or like the barbarian had chosen not to establish such a realm, was not fully human" (Arendt, 1998: 38). The emphasis that Arendt makes on the public sphere, where all human capacities can be realized and perhaps the condition of being called human, is directly related to the importance he gives to the sphere of influence of an action. Here, I understand that the sphere of influence of an action means whether it is open to the public or not. As I have mentioned above, no humanitarian action that has been removed from the public sphere and confined to the private sphere under the guise of privacy can reach its ultimate goal. Here one may asked what the ultimate suit is and why it is necessary. The answer to such a question is quite simple: meaning and approval. An action that is purely implicit to the subject is deprived of meaning. An action that is deprived of meaning cannot have goal like approval. Therefore, the value of an action, at least in terms of the person who performs this action, depends on whether it has been performed as "clear" and "visible". In other words,

> Every activity performed in public can attain an excellence never matched in privacy; for excellence, by definition, the presence of others is always required [...] and that everything that appears in public can be seen and heard by everybody and has the widest possible publicity. For us, appearance—something that is being seen and heard by others as well as by ourselves—constitutes reality. Compared with the reality which comes from being seen and heard, even the greatest forces of intimate life—the passions of the heart, the thoughts of the mind, the delights of the senses—lead an uncertain, shadowy kind of existence unless and until they are transformed, deprivatized and deindividualized, as it were, into a shape to fit them for public appearance (Arendt, 1998: 49–50).

The main argument of the quotation from Arendt is based on "being visible". Being visible binds itself to the principle of autonomous action in order to include the presence of others. In other words, the fact that an action is intrinsic to the actor makes both the actor and the action different, and this difference is bound to be approved in the simplest sense. Here, what I understand from "being approved" is being free of intervention in both legal and moral sense. Hence, the direct relationship between being visible, autonomy, and action goes beyond the public/private distinction of human actions. This connects the people living in the same reality and allows the life and experience imprisoned in *oikos* to appear authentically. In other words, as Arendt claimed,

> Being seen and being heard by others derive their significance from the fact that everybody sees and hears from a different position. This is the meaning of public life, compared to which even the richest and most satisfying family life can offer only the prolongation or multiplication of one's own position with its attending aspects and perspectives. The subjectivity of privacy can be prolonged and multiplied in a family, it can even become so strong that its weight is felt in the public realm; but this family "world" can never replace the reality rising out of the sum total of aspects presented by one object to a multitude of spectators. Only where things can be seen by many in a variety of aspects without changing their identity, so that those who are gathered around them know they see sameness in utter diversity, can worldly reality truly and reliably appear (Arendt, 1998: 56).

As I have mentioned above, the intrinsic coherence of the private and the public includes the meaning of the actions and the approval of the actor. It also corresponds to the reality, which frees the person trapped in the essence of his/ her singular experience from being on his/her own, who does not form his/her connection to the world from only one perspective, and opens the human to a common world. Because, seeing the reality only from one side and to claim that it is understandable only from a single perspective brings the end of the common world, which allows living together (Arendt, 1998: 56–59). Here I would like to emphasize the meaninglessness of a life reduced to one's own singularity and subjectivity. Because, without a separation into public and private spheres, life is an unbroken process. The problem arises from the accounts that dealt each of these complimentary parts in different contexts. When the law, morality and justice cannot completely fulfill this wholeness, when autonomous individuals cannot make themselves visible as a whole, the possibility to live together and to live visible to each other disappears regardless of how the formal framework of life is inclusive. It is impossible to function for the opinions, which deal with the relationship between autonomy and liberty in different context (*negative/positive freedom*), which expresses that individual happiness is left to the individual and the state is not concerned with the happiness of individuals. In this sense, it is necessary to create an area where the principle of autonomy and equality, which is intrinsic to democracy, can blossom itself. But here I do not mention equality between equals and equality between unequal ones. I'm talking about an equality that corresponds to "the original position" expressed by John Rawls. Because equality considered together with justice excludes the concept of equality between classes. This gives autonomous individuals the opportunity to act and manifest themselves without private/public distinction. There must, of course, be conditions for making oneself visible. This presence is, in the simplest sense, possible in a holistic democracy. I comprehend from holistic democracy not only an understanding of democracy that dominates the liberal perspective where everyone has whatever right they have and an equal distribution of rights, but also a democracy where the boundaries of the authority are determined. I suggest that, in other words, in a system where the autonomy principle is interrupted, one can not mention democracy and justice, which is connected to the idea of democracy. Because, autonomy means to have the ability to decide by oneself, and to have the capacity "*to reason self-consciously, to be self-reflective and to be self-determining*" As a condition of having this capacity "persons should enjoy equal rights and, accordingly, equal obligations in the specification of the political framework which generates and limits the opportunities available to them; that is, they should be free and equal in the processes of deliberation about the conditions of their own lives and in the determination of these conditions, so long as they do not deploy this framework to negate the rights of others" (Held, 2006: 274).

Although the autonomy principle expressed by Held covered only individuals in singular terms, this principle can be expanded to the relations between the individuals and groups that I have mentioned at the beginning of the chapter. In this sense, we can say that the autonomy principle is a regulatory principle that connects relations to the notion of justice in terms of laws, ethics and rights. In other words, manifestation of justice itself as a binding principle that goes beyond individual evaluations depends on the manifestation, recognition and approval of each individual or group. Such a condition goes beyond justice, which is meaningful in relation to all other social, political, economic, and moral relations. This also excludes the equality between equals and the equality between the unequal ones, links the equality with the respect to the choices of individuals and groups. However, this respect includes not only respect for others but also for us. In other words, in Dworkin's words, "we must show full respect for the equal objective importance of every person's life but also full respect for our own responsibility to make something valuable of our own life" (Dworkin, 2011: 272).

References

Arendt, Hannah, (1998). *The Human Condition*. London: The University of Chicago Press.

Aristotle, (1992). *The Politics*. (T. A. Sinclair, Trans.). Penguin Books.

Bobbio, Norberto (1989). Democracy and Dictatorship *The Nature and Limits of State Power*. (Peter Kennealy, Trans.). Minneapolis: University of Minnesota Press.

Dworkin, Ronald (2011). *Justice for Hedgehogs*. London: The Belknap Press of Harvard University Press.

Gray, John (2003). *Liberalism*. Minneapolis: The University of Minneapolis University Press.

Habermas, Jurgen (1997). 'The public sphere', in Robert E. Goodin and Philip Pettit (eds) *Contemporary Political Philosophy: An Anthology*, Oxford: Blackwell Publishers

Held, David (2006). *Models of Democracy*, Cambridge: Polity Press

Hobbes, Thomas (1996). *Leviathan*, ed. Richard Tuck Cambridge: Cambridge University Press.

Kant, Immanuel (1991). "On the Common Saying: 'This May be True in Theory, But it Does Not Apply in Practice'," in *Kant: Political Writings*, ed. Raymond Geuss and Quentin Skinner, Cambridge: Cambridge University Press.

Raz, Joseph. (1995). *Ethics in the public domain : essays in the morality of law and politics.* New York: Oxford University Press.

Shields, Christopher (2007). *Aristotle,* London: Routledge

Rosen, Allen D. (1993). *Kant's Theory of Justice,* New York: Cornell University Press.

Weintraub, J (1997). 'The Theory and Politics of the Public/Private Distinction', in J.Weintraub and K.Kumar (eds), *Public and Private in Thought and Practice,* Chicago: University of Chicago Press.

Fulden İbrahimhakkıoğlu

The Affective Epistemology of Ignorance: A Phenomenology of White Unknowing[1]

In his testimony, Darren Wilson, the police officer who shot and killed the 18-year-old Michael Brown, told the grand jury: "[W]hen I grabbed him, the only way I can describe it is I felt like a 5-year-old holding onto Hulk Hogan" (Krishnadev, 2014). The same height as Wilson, Brown had, as Wilson reports, "the most intense aggressive face. The only way I can describe it, it looks like a demon, that's how angry he looked" (Ibid). Based on this testimony, Wilson was exonerated (twice!) of any criminal wrongdoing, by a grand jury as well as the Department of Justice. A year before Brown was killed, George Zimmerman was acquitted of shooting the 17-year-old Trayvon Martin on the grounds that it was self-defense. Zimmerman's testimony must have convinced the jury that Martin, a hoodie wearing young Black man, seemed suspicious and thereby constituted a threat. It was Zimmerman's suspicion that not only defined the meaning of that encounter, but also served to justify the killing in court, whereas Martin's fear as he was being chased by an armed grown man did not seem to count for anything. It was Wilson's fear of Brown, who made him feel completely powerless, insignificant, and vulnerable, despite the fact that Wilson was an armed police officer whereas Brown was an unarmed teenager, which, again, held up in court. Perhaps the jury agreed that they too would have been horrified if they had been in Wilson's or Zimmerman's shoes. In a social context where Black masculinity is codified as inherently threatening and thereby dispensable, it is perhaps easier to empathize with the perpetrators rather than imagining the constant harassment faced by young Black men, who seem to inspire fear and hostility in others simply by virtue of their bodily presence. In this sense, the fear that Wilson's and Zimmerman's testimonies express is hardly peculiar to them, but is instead linked to an affective economy of fear whereby the threat gets attached to particular bodies.

---

1   An earlier version of this essay was presented at SPEP in 2013 in Eugene, Oregon with the title, "Fear, Entitlement, and the Affective Economy of Ignorance," which was subsequently revised and expanded as part of my doctoral dissertation, *The Politics of Paranoia: Affect, Temporality, and the Epistemology of Securitization*, defended in 2016 at the University of Oregon.

Affective economies denote, as Agathangelou et al. put it, "the circulation and mobilization of feelings of desire, pleasure, fear, and repulsion utilized to seduce all of us into the fold of the state – the various ways in which we become invested emotionally, libidinally, and erotically in global capitalism's mirages of safety and inclusion" (Aganthangelou et al., 2008: 122). In other words, a way in which power operates is through the circulation of affect, whose investments shape and situate subjectivity itself. These operations take place on an intimate, bodily level, such that these investments are often enacted pre-reflectively, in that they need not rely on a reflective consciousness. Wilson characterizes Brown as "demonic," for that is the association that arises for him upon the sight of a young, heavyset Black man whom he perceives as threatening. Upon Zimmerman's acquittal, Christopher Myers wrote: "Images matter. They linger in our hearts, vast 'image libraries' that color our actions and ideas, even if we don't recognize them on a conscious level. The plethora of threatening images of young Black people has real-life effects. But if people can see us as young dreamers, boys with hopes and doubts and playfulness, instead of potential threats or icons of societal ills, perhaps they will feel less inclined to kill us" (Myers, 2013). As power works through these affective circuits, the codification of certain bodies as dangerous or threatening suggests a reified positionality in a broader system of meaning that in turn amounts to the dispensability of those bodies. These significations, as affective investments, colonize these encounters by predetermining their meaning and foreclosing other possibilities. Black masculinity becomes that which cannot manifest anything but a threat. When Wilson characterizes Brown as "demonic," his expression is tied to these investments that are linked to an affective economy, by which his perception has been shaped. The meaning of that encounter was predetermined and his exoneration attests to the fact that that meaning is all too self-evident for the court.

The term 'affective economy' suggests that "feelings do not reside in subjects or objects, but are produced as effects of circulation" (Ahmed, 2004: 8). Fear, in this case, is lived both personally, in that it is Wilson's fear felt privately in its pressing urgency, and impersonally, as an element in a circuit of affect, insofar as it is generalized in that it saturates the social field itself, consolidating the misconception that fear is the appropriate reaction to the sight of Black masculinity. One's fear, in this context, is both theirs and not only theirs. Who is to be feared and what shall follow from that fear are constituencies of an affective economy of fear. As John Protevi puts it, "[A]ffect is concretely the imbrication of the social and the somatic, as our bodies change in relation to the changing situations in which they find themselves" (Protevi, 2009: xiv).

Yet, insofar as affect denotes "a body's *capacity* to affect and to be affected" (Gregg & Seigworth, 2010: 2), it highlights relationality or intersubjectivity over subjectivity. Further, since its operation is relational, it always takes place within a particular social and political context. It is my contention that the affective economy of fear does not necessarily respond to a world that has become a more dangerous place, but instead is indicative of the operations of power through the installment of particular circuits of affect and desire. Moreover, while fear serves a self-justifying imperative force, it only does so when claimed by particular subjects who hold epistemic authority in that their claim fits within established affective economies. The potency of the affect stems from its ability to determine the meaning of a situation or an encounter, yet, again, only when claimed by certain subjects.

The killings of young Black men are not named "murder" in that the fear felt by the shooters trump that of the victims. Fear, in this case, serves to define a situation by means of a distortion such that it is not only linked to judgment but also to epistemic authority. After all, it is not *anyone's* fear that determines the meaning of that encounter. It matters whose fear counts and whose does not. For this reason, the effects of fear as an affective economy must be taken up in conjunction with the epistemic practices with which it is bound up. It is only through this connection, through an understanding of fear as linked to an affective epistemology, would one be able to analyze the process whereby certain bodies are codified as threatening. The reason I've chosen to focus on fear in particular is how salient it becomes in intersubjective encounters, as opposed to, say, anxiety, which may be subtler and persistent, and not necessarily linked to a particular object. In the following, I look at how the fear of Black bodies serves as a self-justifying mechanism for the infliction of violence. I offer a phenomenological analysis of white ignorance that manifests itself through the fear of racialized bodies. Fear (and the violence that it serves to justify) here is indicative of internalized racism based upon a coding of Black masculinity as threatening, a coding that is historically contingent and without a basis in reality. As Angela Davis puts it, "[T]he development of new ways of thinking about racism requires us not only to understand economic, social, and ideological structures, but also collective psychic structures" (Davis, 2016: 89). For this purpose, I offer this analysis as an example of how a politics of paranoia operates on an intersubjective level by means of an affective economy. The paranoid epistemological framework is used here to justify the dispensability of the marked bodies as fear justifies violence, as can be seen in the trial of Zimmerman, which hinged on whether "this young black boy, with his bag of candy and his iced tea and his sweatshirt, was a threat" (Myers, 2013).

I Affective Epistemology of Ignorance

In her famous work *Epistemic Injustice* (2007), Miranda Fricker explores how suspicion is at work in certain epistemic practices. While the question of whose testimony is granted credibility is certainly relevant here, I am more interested in looking at the role of affect itself in epistemic practices. I suggest that there is an affective epistemology at work in the process through which an encounter attains meaning and the determinant affect is that which grabs a hold of the subject who holds epistemic authority. Epistemic authority, in this case, is linked not only to one's social location but also to where one is positioned with regards to an epistemology of ignorance that criminalizes Black masculinity. In other words, when it comes to epistemic justice, it is not only a matter of whose testimony is granted credibility, but also a matter of whose affective disposition determines the meaning of the encounter, depending on where that disposition fits within the social imaginary.

The imperative force entailed by paranoiac epistemic practices undoubtedly has a colonial history, which is decisive in whose fear shall count, whose paranoia shall be granted epistemic legitimacy, and whose affective predisposition gets to determine the meaning of an encounter. The epistemological framework that undergirds the politics of paranoia is still very much shaped by what Nelson Maldonado-Torres calls "Manichean misanthropic skepticism." This "permanent suspicion," born in the sixteenth century, is "a form of questioning the very humanity of colonized peoples" (Maldonado-Torres, 2007: 245). "Misanthropic skepticism," Maldonado-Torres writes, "provides the basis for the *preferential option for the ego conquiro*, which explains why security for some can conceivably be obtained at the expense of the lives of others" (Maldonado-Torres, 2007: 246). What underlies the dehumanization and the related dispensability of the peoples of darker races, for Maldonado-Torres, is this deep suspicion that is decisive in who is dispensable, whose status as human is suspect, who fully counts as human, and also, perhaps most relevant for our purposes, whose fear is granted legitimacy.

The suspicion and fear that are expressed by the perpetrators (and legitimized by the court) in these trials are systemically linked to questions about biopower, about whose life counts. As African-Americans are deemed dispensable per Manichean misanthropic skepticism, the Black Lives Matter movement emerged as "an ideological and political intervention in a world where Black lives are systematically and intentionally targeted for demise," to celebrate those lives, affirm their humanity, and seek "resilience in the face of deadly oppression" ("Guiding Principles," *Black Lives Matter*). While I focus on these two trials in particular, it is worth noting that these are by no means isolated instances but are instead indicative of a larger structure of anti-Black racism entrenched in and perpetuated by practices of policing. As Angela Davis points out, we must, at the same time, attend to "the way in which anti-Muslim racism has really thrived on the foundation of anti-Black racism" (Davis, 2016: 39) in the United States, as both operate through an affective economy of fear that deems particular bodies to be threatening and thereby dispensable. It is also worth noting that the police brutality against women of color, and especially trans women of color, receives even less attention, as the mainstream media often exclusively depicts men as the victims. The Say Her Name movement seeks to render visibility for those Black women who are the victims of anti-Black police brutality. While police brutality against both Black men and women is linked to larger questions about biopower, about whose life matters, who counts as human, and who is deemed dispensable, there is a gender difference in that it is often Black men who are codified as particularly threatening as a justification for their violability. As much as I do not wish to erase those women who are the victims of anti-Black violence, in the following I focus particularly on the codification of Black masculinity as threatening, given that my interest lies in examining the workings of fear as demonstrative of an affective epistemology. In this sense, I attend to these killings at the intersection of race and gender: Black masculinity as the object of fear within a racialized affective economy.

In the case of Martin, it was the hoodie that he wore paired with his black skin that rendered him suspicious in the eyes of Zimmerman. Though it would be a worthwhile effort to give a genealogical account of the hoodie as an article of clothing that came to be associated with dangerous Black masculinity, I am more interested in how that signification persists in the social imaginary such that it serves as a justification of violence. There is an epistemology of ignorance at work in that a myth (the myth of the dangerous Black man with a hoodie) passes for knowledge. Zimmerman's suspicion and fear are indicative of a larger system of meaning in which Black masculinity is codified as threatening and thereby must be annihilated. Even though that codification itself is based on myth rather than reality, it continues to serve as a justification for the killing of young Black men. Charles Mills's account of the epistemology of ignorance is pertinent here, yet one must consider it as a kind of epistemology that is linked to an affective economy (of fear, in particular) – in other words, an affective epistemology. Mills argues that ignorance is a "structural group-based miscognition" (Mills, 2007: 13). It is understood not simply as an epistemic gap or a lack, but rather a mechanism that reproduces and sustains the oppression of marginalized groups. In this sense, ignorance is systematic, socially sanctioned, and productive.[2] It is invested with power in that it both conceals and upholds the privileges of dominating groups, as well as the oppression of marginalized groups. White ignorance, like other "group-based cognitive handicap(s)" (Mills, 2007: 15) is productive insofar as it passes for knowledge in creating an epistemic hegemony based on "*white misunderstanding, misrepresentation, evasion, and self-deception on matters related to race*" (Mills, 1997: 19 emphasis in the original). While Zimmerman identifies as Latino, this does not make him immune to this epistemic hegemony, for "white ignorance" does not take its name by virtue of the fact that all those who subscribe to it are white, but because it is the product of a social order whose beneficiaries are whites as a group. While not all those who suffer from this "miscognition" are whites, not all whites suffer from it either. Regardless, the term *white ignorance* refers to a condition that is structurally sustained where distortions on matters surrounding race serve as knowledge, as this takes place in a white supremacist political context.

Ignorance, in this way, denotes an epistemic hegemony based on the appropriation of facts through various means including willful misinterpretation, evasion, distortion, and shrouding. It is an outcome of the Europeanization of epistemic norms, a process whose roots can be traced back to colonialism, whereby the forms of knowing that do not fit into European standards are marginalized, if not completely eliminated. It is the case, then, that the white epistemic norm not only establishes mass hallucination on matters of race by way of obscuring facts, but also entails a violent omission of non-European ways of knowing. Further, ignorance of this kind, far from indicating a mere naïveté on part of the members of the dominant groups, names an integral part of white subjectivity today.

In this sense, ignorance may represent something more expansive than a simple cognitive handicap, as subjects act on, abide by, and live their lives by virtue of the kind of ignorance that passes for knowledge under such epistemic hegemony. Ignorance could be further scrutinized as a constitutive component of white subjectivities. My purpose here is to offer an analysis of ignorance as not only a cognitive phenomenon, but an embodied practice. Ignorance as a systemically sustained condition, which endorses white domination, is repeatedly enacted by epistemic agents in the form of mistaken knowledge, whereby

---

2   Systematic and socially sanctioned, because ignorance is both backed up and practiced on a structural level; and productive, because it produces and reproduces racism as well as its subjects.

it establishes its full meaning in embodied practices and shapes the agents' embodied subjectivity.

Mills characterizes the epistemology of ignorance as *"an inverted episte-mology"* (Mills, 1997: 19) that relies on a distorted moral psychology, or as he puts it, "white moral cognitive dysfunction" (Mills, 1997: 95). As such, ignorance and the "moral cognitive distortion" it involves "can potentially be studied by the new research program of cognitive science" (Ibid). Thus, for Mills, white ignorance is, first and foremost, "a cognitive phenomenon" (Mills, 2007: 20). Subjects of racism, then, are taken up as "cognizers," and the dysfunctions of their perception, conception, and memory, among other things, are what need to be examined.[3] However, as Mills' interlocutors as well as other feminist and anti-racist work on ignorance have shown, this cognitive based approach does not exhaust the meaning of ignorance (Bailey, 2007; Ortega, 2006; Townley, 2006; Sullivan, 2006). In order to grasp the extent to which ignorance of this kind achieves its full meaning, the ways in which it finds entrenchment in the body as a part of bodily knowing within a racist social context must be explored. Such investigation will shed light on not only the ways in which ignorance is embodied or rather, embedded in the body, but also how ignorance becomes a constituent of white subjectivity, precisely in this very embodiment. Since ignorance denotes a *specific* way of knowing (that is distorted, skewed, or false) and acts as "knowledge" under the given truth regime, "knowledge" which is in fact ignorance will be indicated in quotation marks in the rest of this essay.

II The Embodiment of Racialized Ignorance

The question of the body has a special place in matters of race, for it is the racially marked body that is subjugated. Perhaps when Merleau-Ponty announced, "I am my body," he overlooked the condition that some of us are *more* his or her body than others, and that this is by no means a pleasant or a liberating experience, but rather a thoroughly violent one, under the normative white gaze. As many feminist and anti-racist works have shown, the aesthetic dimension, how the body is *seen* by others, has everything to do with how the body is lived and *can be* lived. The black body is lived, for example, according to Lewis Gordon, "as a form of human deficiency" (Gordon, 1999: 101). As the body is objectified under the white gaze, it becomes a *thing*, from which one is distanced (Yancy, 2008: 15). It is this experience of objectification Fanon had in mind when he

---

3   This is what Mills undertakes in his article "White Ignorance."

wrote: "I came into this world anxious to uncover the meaning of things, my soul desirous to be at the origin of the world, and *here I am an object among other objects*" (Fanon, 2008: 89). The body under the white gaze is the racially marked body that is always overdetermined and impeded in its objectification. The marked subject seeking transcendence is distanced from h/er body, which s/he experiences as a burden whereby h/er status as a constituting subject is rendered problematic as s/he lives h/er subjectivity as always already restricted. Whereas the unmarked subject experiences no discrepancy between how h/er body is seen and lived, thereby h/er status as "the origin of the world" eludes any sort of problematization.

One's embodiment becomes an issue precisely when one's body is *marked*. Thus, it makes sense for us to take the body as a site of political contestation, as so many times one's capabilities as a human being are reduced to one's body, or rather what that body signifies. Further, many feminists and anti-racists have made the point that we not only *are* our marked bodies, but we *become* them in perpetually adopting and inhabiting the meanings that our bodies carry. This is demonstrated by Iris Young in her examination of the physical timidity of feminine bodily comportment:

> Typically, the feminine body underuses its real capacity, both as the potentiality of its physical size and strength and as the real skills and coordination which are available to it. Feminine bodily existence is an inhibited intentionality, which simultaneously reaches toward a projected end with an 'I can' and withholds its full bodily commitment to that end in a self-imposed 'I cannot.' (Young, 1980: 146)

The feminine body *learns* to be timid through its interaction with the world, and it "knows" that it is "a thing which exists as *looked at and acted upon*" (Young, 1980: 148) as opposed to a fully capable agent of action. Hence the feminine body *becomes* a fragile body through habituation, and enacts the fragility that it became. The "knowledge" that the feminine body acquires (that it is weak and fragile) is a piece of knowledge that interferes with the achievement of the full potentiality of that body.

When thinking about white ignorance, the issue lies more within the embodiment of the privileged than the oppressed, in other words, within those who are unburdened by a body that carries with it the mark of inferiority. Merleau-Ponty's philosophy of the body as the primary site of subjectivity can offer a way to understand the construction of white subjectivities through an epistemology of ignorance. Merleau-Ponty writes: "Bodily experience forces us to acknowledge an imposition of meaning, which is not the work of a universal-constituting consciousness, a meaning which clings to certain contents" (Merleau-Ponty,

1962: 46). This imposed meaning is an accumulation of the body's interaction with the environment, through which the body *learns*. Thus, based on this give-and-take relation, one may characterize this interaction as some sort of a transaction with the world, a process through which the world comes to inhabit the body as much as the body inhabits the world. In his famous phantom limb example, Merleau-Ponty explains that the patient still acts as if he is not missing a limb, even though he is perfectly aware on a reflective level that he cannot perform certain tasks in the way he used to be able to. He attempts to open the door by way of turning the doorknob, yet the doorknob cannot be turned as he is missing his arm. From this, we can infer that his "habitual body" involves the implicit knowledge that one is to turn a doorknob in order to open the door. The habitual body is comprised of the sedimentation of such knowledge whereby the body acts on the environment based on that knowledge, with no necessary awareness on a reflective level. As the conditions of sedimentation change (as in the case of losing a limb), the ways in which the body acts on the world will gradually change (that is, the subject will eventually develop new habits to adjust to the changing circumstances). Thus, the subject can learn to inhabit the world otherwise.

Merleau-Ponty's insight about the body as the site of knowledge offers a means through which we can examine the sedimentation of ignorance in the body. As white subjectivities are shaped through bodily interactions with a racist world, the accumulation of "knowledge" that is sedimented in one's habitual body will involve the kind of "knowledge" that is wrong, deceiving, and detrimental. Taken alongside Mills's account of the epistemology of ignorance, this suggests that the body *knows*, yet what it knows is the ignore-ance of white privilege which gets passed on as knowledge under the current truth regime. The codification of the Black (and Brown) masculine bodies as threatening is precisely linked to this process of sedimentation, where the body reacts in fear in that encounter, regardless of whether or not there is real threat.

What the body knows, the body takes for granted. No reflective awareness need be directed toward that "knowledge," nonetheless the "knowledge" itself is enacted continuously. If we were to take up this phenomenon as a way of accounting for white subjectivities whose racial experience is not marked (thereby the body is not lived as a burden), we can see the ways in which ignorance is acquired through bodily habituation and sedimentation, and in turn enacted without reflective awareness. Such ignorance that is embedded in one's body and enacted in one's bodily engagements with the world is a critical component of the epistemology of ignorance.

In order to see how this plays out in a racialized context, one may consider Fanon's account of the body schema. The implicit knowledge that is sedimented in the body is at play in Fanon's depiction of reaching for cigarettes as well. If he wants to smoke, all he needs to do is to stretch his arm to pick up the pack of cigarettes at the other end of the table. And to light the cigarette, he would need to open the drawer where the matches are. He suggests that he performs these moves by virtue of an "implicit knowledge" (Fanon, 2008: 90), as his body moves around space based on this very knowledge that it acquired over time. What Merleau-Ponty calls "habitual body," then, is linked with Fanon's "body schema," which he defines as "[a] slow construction of myself as a body in a spatial and temporal world" (Fanon, 2008: 91). Similar to Merleau-Ponty's account of the habitual body, the body schema in this context denotes a free transaction between the body and the world, a transaction that Fanon calls "a genuine dialectic,"[4] through which "a definitive structuring of myself and the world" takes place (Ibid). Yet, beneath this body schema, according to Fanon, there emerges a "historical-racial schema," whereby the racially marked body is "woven…out of a thousand details, anecdotes, and stories" (Ibid), which interrupts and indeed renders impossible a free transaction between a racist world and a racially marked subject. The historical-racial schema is marked by a violent imposition whereby "white people's racist perceptions of [Fanon] as a savage subperson" (Sullivan, 2006: 102) (i.e. white ignorance) demand to be incorporated into the body schema. This marks a break down in the free flow of the body schema, instead "giving way to an epidermal racial schema." (Fanon, 2008: 91). In the context of racism, then, a "race-neutral"[5] body schema is shattered and superseded by the historical-racial schema, which debases and restrains the racially marked body in substantial ways.

---

4   Fanon explains genuineness as the absence of "imposition." Even though there is imposition in Merleau-Ponty's account, it is important to note that Fanon and Merleau-Ponty uses "imposition" in a different way. For Fanon, it denotes the world "determining" the body, whereas for Merleau-Ponty there is no such determination, but instead a set of constraints imposed onto the body.

5   Even though this is how Fanon puts it, we may question what racially neutral means in this context (especially in the all-pervasiveness of racism), and whether the historical-racial schema is, as it were, superimposed. We may also ask whether this free-flow, or true dialectic, is in fact a real condition, granted that our embodiment is always already constrained in different ways by virtue of being shaped through the world. For example, what Fanon takes to be a neutral, standard body schema may very well be a masculine one, taking itself to be natural and concealing its own history achieved through masculine entitlement.

Shannon Sullivan sums up this situation in the following way: "In a world infused with white privilege, a black person's bodily comportment is always being constituted by the raced and racist space in which he or she lives" (Sullivan, 2006: 103). By implication, the white body schema is taken as "normal," as that which eludes or remains uninterrupted by the detrimental effects of the historical-racial schema. However, this situation is problematic, for the white body schema that is shaped by racism is not "normal" or "standard" by any means, but normative and standardized, and one may even add, pathological.[6] Sullivan attempts to mitigate this problem by explaining that "the lack of racialized obstacles to the formation of white person's body schema exists precisely because of the historico-racial schema that privileges whiteness," whereby "[t]he same historico-racial schema described by Fanon both disrupts the black person's and enables the white person's composition of their bodily schemas" (Sullivan, 2006: 103). Thus, for instance, white cleanliness/purity and Black dangerousness/criminality are established in the same move when whites immediately lock their car doors upon the sight of a Black person approaching (Yancy, 2012: 31).

Even though this approach to the white body schema/black historical-racial schema as bound up with each other is helpful in understanding racially differentiated forms of lived bodily experience, it lacks precision in its failure to specify modes of racist embodiment, as white embodiment is simply seen in terms of a *lack* of impediment. Yet, if we are to take up ignorance as a positive notion that is productive of subjectivity, we are compelled to address the specific modes in which it is embodied. Only then these modes can be de-naturalized by exposing how the white body schema is a function of a system of racial oppression. In other words, it is not that the white body schema is simply uninhibited and the non-white body schema is, but rather that they are both impacted by the historical-racial schema. If we were to make an analogy, we could say that the uninhibited masculine body cannot be understood as simply a diametrical opposition of the impeded feminine body as explicated by Young, but rather it involves its own modes of motility and comportment. This difference can be observed, for instance, in pubescent schoolchildren. Girls tend keep their legs closed, have a modest posture, they hunch over to hide their breasts, and so on. Boys, on the other hand, have a much more "expansive" posture as they stretch their legs, keep their shoulders up, and move around and fidget. It would be

---

6   Pathological' insofar as the uninhibited, entitled white body schema is enabled by the historical-racial (racist?) schema. That is to say, it is pathologically racist.

wrong to assume that the masculine comportment, in this case, is natural or ideal, whereas the feminine comportment is simply its impediment, as we very well know that not all aspects of this expansive comportment is desirable or ideal (for instance, bullying or even just crowding others). The question, then, is whether one can pinpoint an analogue of these masculine modes of embodiment as inhabitation of gender in white embodiment of ignorance.

Racialized modes of ignorance, I would like to suggest, are the functions of sedimented "knowledge" of bodies. What the body "knows" and enacts based on that "knowledge," in this model, is white ignorance. While it is not only white bodies that enact that "knowledge," whose schema is shaped by the sedimentation of ignorance as mistaken knowledge, that "knowledge" that is enacted itself is situated in a white supremacist social context. In this sense, regardless of one's particular subjective position, there is a certain complicity, an internalization of whiteness as it were, at work in the enactment of that "knowledge." However, given that I am interested in bringing out the peculiarity of that which is rendered invisible in its universality, normativity, and unmarked status, I shall work with the specific example of the white body in order to map the impact of historical-racial schema onto the white body schema. In this sense, the project at hand is similar to that of Peggy McIntosh's in her essay "White Privilege," where she enumerates the ways in which whites are privileged, yet at the same time are blind to those privileges. Once pinned down, the unthought dimension of the body may be transformed.

Caroline Knowles's account of race as "made through corporeality and comportment, through bodily movement and intersections with space" (Knowles 2010: 31) may prove helpful to map out the ways in which whiteness is *made* as a specific mode of corporeality and comportment. She notes that the "[t]echniques of the body, posture, attitude, movements and habits are also performances of ethnicity, race and hybridised cultural practices which lend their (orchestrated) mobile character to the architecture of the streets" (Ibid). Thus, by looking at "how people comport themselves," one can gain insight into "both enactment and composition of (raced) subjectivity" (Ibid). This way, modes of embodiment that are marked by whiteness do not go unnoticed. She notes, "[r]outine corporeality and comportment also intersect with entitlement and territory," as whites "walk with a sense of (historical) entitlement, an unchallengeable right to be there" in cities and towns where whites historically have resided (Knowles 2010: 32). White entitlement, here, corresponds to feelings of discomfort, fear, and vigilance on the part of non-whites. According to Sara Ahmed, this territorialization is linked to "the regulation of bodies in space through the uneven distribution of fear" (Ahmed, 2004: 70). Thus, spaces that become territories are "claimed as rights by some bodies and not others" (Ibid). As the public spaces are territorialized as masculine, for example, Elizabeth Stanko (1990) explains that feminine bodies are produced as fearful and restricted mobility. Vulnerability, then, far from being "an inherent characteristic of women's bodies," is "an effect that works to secure femininity as a delimitation of movement in the public, and over-inhabitance in the private" (Ahmed, 2004: 70).

This dyadic affective economy of entitlement/fear transforms the body schema so that the social space is arranged in a certain manner. Fear, Ahmed notes, "involves shrinking the body" (Ahmed, 2004: 69) so that the body takes up less space, turns inward, tightens up, seals onto itself. Entitlement, on the other hand, is lived as uninhibited "movement or expansion," causing the Other to feel fear as a restricted body (Ibid). Just as masculine entitlement is bound up with feminine fear and vulnerability, white entitlement (not as mere lack of inhibition but as expansion) precipitates fear and vulnerability in those who are not white, and thus are not welcome in white spaces.[7]

Yet, one may suggest that whites do not always experience their bodies as expansive, entitled bodies in relation to disadvantaged non-whites. What about, one may ask, when whites find themselves fearful, in what they perceive as a dangerous situation in their encounter with non-whites, for instance, sitting in their car in a Black neighborhood? What does fear do, in such cases? Does it involve a shrinking of the body to give way to uninhibited Black expansion?

White vulnerability, in such cases, operates as an oppressive mechanism against non-whites in its consolidation of white purity and innocence, for white purity and innocence are established only in relation to Black criminality. There is an insidious feeling of entitlement at work in white fear. We must ask who gets to fear, whose fear is legitimized, under what conditions, and at the expense of whom. In one of the very first scenes of the provocative 2005 film *Crash*, in which racial dynamics in Los Angeles are explored, a white woman holds her husband tight upon the sight of two Black men. This is noticed by one of these men who goes on to tell his friend:

> Man, look around you, man. You couldn't find a whiter, safer, better lit part of the city right now. But yet this white woman sees two Black guys who look like UCLA students strolling down the sidewalk and her reaction is blind fear? I mean, look at us dog, are we dressed like gangbangers? Huh? No. Do we look threatening? No. Fact: if anybody

---

7   Jackson Katz gives an account of how masculinity offers a sense of empowerment to men of color in his reading of the media depictions of masculinity in his documentary *Tough Guise*. This offers an interesting way to think about how racial domination and gender domination are linked.

should be scared around here, it's us. We're the only two Black faces surrounded by a sea of over-caffeinated white people, patrolled by the triggerhappy LAPD. So you tell me: Why aren't we scared?[8]

Affective economy of fear operates in such a way that renders irrational, racist fear of whites legitimate. This kind of fear reinforces "the stability of white identity qua normative" (Yancy, 2012: 31), while consolidating the Black identity as the dangerous, inferior Other. White fear, then, is linked to entitlement insofar as whites are entitled to feel fear, even when they are in a safe white space, i.e. white territory, whereas non-whites have to deal with the consequences of this fear.[9] Fear is also a bodily expression, a symptom, of white ignorance. It enacts a certain knowledge claim, or a series of knowledge claims that not only permeate one's cognitive states, but are also operative in one's bodily comportment, in that one's comportment is shaped through fear. Thus, upon the sight of a man of color, white people act upon this "knowledge" ("Black is dangerous," "Black is criminal," "The Black is going to kill me," "The Black is going to rob me," and so on) that is sedimented in their habitual body. In reacting with fear, the body "knows" Black criminality, and responds immediately based on that "knowledge."

White fear, then, is not a kind of fear that shrinks the white body, but instead, it shrinks the Black body. This is not only because the white body shames, degrades, and expels the Black body in fearing, but also because white fear becomes a real, and sometimes fatal, threat. White fear not only violates and degrades, but also kills Black bodies, which it takes as its object. Hence, vulnerability is displaced: a Black body is the truly vulnerable body when confronted with an entitled, fearful white body. Ahmed notes that while affect involves "readings of openness of bodies to being affected," fear in particular "reads that openness as the possibility of danger or pain," as opposed to hope, which "reads that openness as the possibility of desire or joy" (Ahmed, 2004: 185). This particular reading projected onto Black masculinity that anticipates harm is linked to an affective epistemology wherein fear performs white ignorance, in the form of mistaken knowledge. Ahmed writes: "These readings reshape bodies. Whilst fear may shrink the body in anticipation of injury, hope may expand the contours of bodies, as they reach towards what is possible" (Ibid). Yet this

---

8   It must be noted that right after giving this speech, this man goes on to pull out a gun and hijack a car. It later becomes clear that he sees his own criminality not simply as a reproduction of a stereotype, but instead an act of resistance in the face of racism. The film was clearly going for the shock value with this scene.

9   In fact, toward the end of the film, one of these men gets killed as a result of a white man's fear.

particular economy of fear, in contrast, expands the body that is positioned vis-à-vis Black masculinity in its anticipation of injury. This expansion takes place both in the infliction of violence and the legitimization of that violence within juridical settings. The fearing body may experience oneself as vulnerable, as the to-be victim. That experience, and not that of the actual victim, is what counts in trial. That possibility of harm, that perception of danger is decidedly the sole perspective through which adjudication takes place, where a racialized logic of preemption is operative. Fear determines the meaning of the encounter in its linked to an affective epistemology of ignorance.

In an act of reversal, fear shrinks the racially marked body, while expanding the non-marked body. Within the rhetoric of safety, "We want our streets to be safe" so often reads, "We want only good white folks on these streets." The little boy who thinks that Fanon is going to "eat him" is afraid, and his fear reconfigures Fanon's body by reshaping its comportment: "My body was returned to me spread-eagled, disjointed, redone, draped in mourning..." (Fanon, 2008: 93). Fanon begins trembling with fear felt as coldness, misread by the little boy as rage. Fanon cannot be trembling with *fear*, as Blacks do not fear: fear is a privilege reserved to whites; it is a white prerogative to fear a Black man and end his life on the basis of that fear. Whites are entitled to be vulnerable, in their enactment of ignorance, which operates through fear as an embodied "knowledge" that "Blacks are dangerous." This very "knowledge" that fear conveys establishes white subjectivity in the form of purity.

Ahmed notes that "[f]ear's relation to the object has an important temporal dimension" (Ahmed, 2004: 65). As a felt intensity in the present, fear "projects us from the present into a future," through "an *anticipation* of hurt of injury" (Ibid). That very anticipation rests on an overdetermination of the fear's object ("Black as evil," "Black as dangerous"), rather than a felt anxiety that comes from uncertainty ("What is that stranger going to do to me?"). There is a paranoiac epistemology at work as the encounter is overdetermined by the possibility of injury. There is a presumption on the part of the subject of fear that s/he is going to be hurt, or harmed in some way. This presumption is linked to bodily ignorance, insofar as the overdetermination that is imposed on the fear object is that which the body "knows." In this sense, fear is not only a projection of the present into the future by way of anticipating hurt, but a culmination of the past sedimented knowledge of the body which make up that very anticipation. The temporal continuum of fear thereby shows that fear is not a "natural" reaction of the body, but is linked to the epistemology of ignorance that one embodies. Fear, then, is the performance of that ignorance, and as such, it involves a certain disclosure: it is the disclosing of one's own status as an oppressor to oneself. It is this disclosure that we do not find in the undisrupted modes of white embodiment[10] whereby ignorance prevails. Yet in the disruption of the body schema by the previously concealed historical-racial schema emerges the very possibility to undo that "whiteliness," to borrow from Marilyn Frye, in the form of white ignorance.

It is important to note that fear is not the only affect through which white ignorance is expressed, but there are milder forms that are just as expressive, as shall be shown through a reading of an episode of the situational comedy television series, *The New Adventures of Old Christine*. These include distress, anxiety, discomfort, unease, and apprehension, among others, all of which are tied to racial entitlement in varying degrees.

III Whiteness Embodied: The Case of Christine

The New Adventures of Old Christine is a television series that ran from 2006 to 2010. It is a comedy about the life of a white single mother Christine (Julia Louis-Dreyfus) after her divorce. She owns a gym with her best friend/business partner Barb (Wanda Sykes). Unlike the majority of white American sitcom characters portrayed as "good whites," Christine's whiteness and egalitarian commitments are repeatedly problematized throughout the show. Numerous episodes expose and deal with Christine's ignorant progressivism, and one in particular ("White Like Me") takes up Christine's insidious racism lurking behind her self-proclaimed colorblindness. In this episode, Barb gets featured in a business journal about Black women, hoping to get new members in the gym. As soon as the interview is published, Christine finds that the gym is crowded with new members, all of whom are Black women. Upon her brother and ex-husband's visit, she looks unusually busy and stressed out. Her brother, amused by the change in the demographics of the clientele, comments, "You own a Black gym!" to which Christine responds, "What? Where did you get that?" and goes on to say that of course she has not noticed that everyone in the gym is Black, because she is "a Democrat." "What does that mean?" her ex-husband asks, to which she responds: "I drive a Prius. I don't see color."

Christine's self-proclaimed colorblindness is in direct conflict with her feelings of discomfort around the new Black female members of the gym. Her responses to her brother and ex-husband's questions regarding this are short and dismissive. She looks highly tense and uncomfortable, as her ex-husband and her brother continue asking her questions. "What color is your Prius?" her

---

10 For instance, comfort, complacency, and entitlement that comes with "whiteliness," to borrow from Marilyn Frye.

brother asks, mocking her "colorblindness." Christine responds: "No idea. I'm not a racist." When her ex-husband tries to explain that it does not make her a racist to *notice* that somebody is Black, she snaps and says that she does not want to talk about this anymore. As her brother asks, "What's wrong with you, you're so stressed out, it's like the muscles in your jaw are so tight, you're developing a tick," the camera turns to Christine whose eye started twitching.

What causes Christine's unusual stress is not revealed, at least not until the next day. Barb, having been overwhelmed by having to deal with everything by herself asks Ali (the socially awkward white gym worker who seems to be rather enjoying the change in the gym as she is dancing to the stereotypically Black music) where Christine is. Ali points at Christine's office, where we see Christine staring through the glass door at the new members with an uneasy look on her face. Barb gets Christine to come out and help out with the signing up process for two new members. As Christine is introduced to them, her comportment gives away that she feels very uncomfortable. As they carry on an awkward conversation in which Christine makes little sense, Christine's eye starts twitching again. When Barb asks, "What's going on with your face," Christine responds, "Equality… Hope…" She cannot wait to flee the situation. She finally says, "Now if you will just excuse me, I will pop black into my office." She pauses, embarrassed because of her slip of the tongue, and corrects herself, "Back. Not black," nervously laughing. She goes on to make things worse saying, "So if you'll excuse me, I will be white black."

Christine's feelings of unease are precipitated by her close proximity to Black women, which makes absolutely no sense to her. Her upper middle class suburban life style and egalitarian values (such as driving an environment-friendly car, sending her son to a posh private school, always being surrounded by white people, etc.) hitherto had been able to mask her white ignorance.[11] Her body is signaling something that Christine had been ignorant about and is reluctant to face: her own racism. Here we have a case of white ignorance exposed through bodily discomfort: twitching, nervous laughter, and slips of the tongue. White ignorance can be lived unproblematically insofar as one keeps one's distance from non-whites – which is why my students often tell me, they have never really had to think about race because there were no people of color in the town where they grew up, as if whiteness constitutes a racially "blank slate." Christine's body schema, then, is enabled precisely by the historical-racial schema: a body

---

11   That is, insofar as she is ignore-ant of her own privileged status precisely by virtue of being ignore-ant of others.

unrestricted, entitled, and oblivious, unaware that its lack of restriction comes at the expense of others' suffering.[12] This is revealed by the disruption of her bodily schema, which leaves her feel threatened, in distress, and confused.

Christine's case makes it clear that it is not so much that the white body is untouched by the historical-racial schema, but rather, that the modes of its comportment are racially differentiated, namely, comfort/discomfort, extension/shrinkage, complacency/fear, arrogance/distress… Whereas the first end of the spectrum entails a forgetting, denial, and ignore-ance of white privilege (while at the same time benefitting from it to the extent of abuse), the second end denotes a problematized state of white ignorance whereby the body enacts, consolidates, and discloses its own ignorance. Further, the two ends of the spectrum are inherently tied to one other, as white complacency, arrogance, and ignorance are bound up with white fear, discomfort, and feelings of unease.

George Yancy (2008a) calls the disclosure of one's own racism (be it through affective forms such as fear, or otherwise) enabled by the disruption of white body schema, "white ambush." Whiteness, not a physiological trait, but a social becoming for Yancy, entails an embodiment of racism in a racist society. The ways in which racism is "embedded within one's embodied habitual engagement with the social world and how it is weaved within the unconscious, impacting everyday mundane transactions" (Yancy, 2008a: 230) lead to experiencing whiteness as ambush, precisely because one catches oneself off-guard, realizes one's ignorance, and undergoes a certain estrangement and distancing from oneself. Yancy suggests that these moments of ambush are manifestations of one's own racism that had gone unnoticed, and they may become the occasion for self-transformation. If white ignorance is mistaken, racially motivated, skewed knowledge that is sedimented in the white habitual body thereby comprising the white body schema, the very undoing of that ignorance will involve "performing the body's racialized interactions with the world differently" (Yancy, 2008b: 843), rather than merely a cognitive shift.

The necessity for such transformation becomes clear in the case of Christine, where Christine does not *believe* that she is racist or that Blacks do not belong in her gym, yet her body still reacts to being in close proximity to Black women. Attending to her feeling of discomfort, Christine admits to Barb, "For the last two days every time I walk into this gym, I feel nervous…I just want to hide

---

12 Various effects of racial marginalization exemplify this suffering. Christine's body schema (i.e. white bodily ignorance) conceal both this marginalization and her own privilege (for she does not have to deal with it so long as she holds egalitarian beliefs – yet her body reveals the racism embedded within).

in my office and not talk to anyone. Do you have any idea what it's like to be a minority?" Barb, of course, as a Black woman, very well knows "what it's like to be a minority," about which Christine is clueless. Yet, the issue is neutralized in Barb's attempt to comfort Christine that she is not a racist by saying, "Everyone feels more comfortable when they are surrounded by people who look like them. That's why Martha Stewart bought Connecticut."

Except, of course, that white discomfort is linked to a very specific history of white racism, and finds embodiment as a form of white entitlement. It is not the case that *any* white person in Christine's situation would feel uncomfortable, either: Christine's discomfort at the gym contrasts with Ali's enhanced comfort. Rather than dealing with her racist sentiments and looking for ways to undo them, Christine decides to "integrate" the gym by getting white people to sign up, so that she would feel more comfortable around "people who look like [her]." The disruption of her body schema as a disclosure of her whiteliness is suspended as Christine goes back to her blissful ignorance and white complacency. Returning to her comfort zone, she refuses to attend to her own affective states as symptoms of the problematic manner in which she inhabits whiteness. The possibility of inhabiting whiteness otherwise is foreclosed upon the decision to ignore her body and bodily ignorance. There is, of course, another path to take. Instead of going back to blissful ignorance, one may choose to spend time with one's own distress and retrain one's body to employ other modes in the encounter with the Other, namely, wonder, curiosity, openness, sympathy, generosity, and so on. This involves an ethics of self-transformation, which has been articulately explicated by a number of scholars (Lugones, 1987; Mahmood, 2005).

In this context, ignorance, conceptualized as a positive notion, is productive of white subjectivity, rather than being its deficient aftereffect. As seen in the white person's encounter with the Other, fear operates as an oppressive mechanism that not only degrades, expels, and shames Blackness (and inhibits the Black body schema), but also establishes white subjectivity as purity, innocence, and moral superiority. In this sense, there is an affective economy in which fear partakes whereby white bodily comportment is marked by entitlement. When the white subject experiences fear, s/he experiences h/er own ignorance as distorted, sedimented, embodied "knowledge." Fear, then, marks a disclosure whereby the white body schema is threatened and disrupted, and this disruption can potentially become the occasion for self-transformation as undoing whiteness. As seen in the character of Christine, a white woman with egalitarian values, one's body can enact sedimented white ignorance despite one's own personal or political commitments. This experience of one's ignorance expressed through bodily comportment and affectivity offers insight into forms of white ignorance that are irreducible to a cognitive framework that prioritizes cognitive states over embodied practices. By attending to these bodily reactions, the ways in which ignorance is a bodily inhabitation can be explored. Such exploration could provide a basis for the transformation of the body schema and the affective economy at work in such encounters in a racialized context. These crossings between phenomenology and social epistemology elicit important tools in the service of dismantling systems of oppression, on which they shed light.

References

Agathangelou, Anna M., Bassichis, M. Daniel, Spira Tamara L. (2008). "Intimate Investments: Homonormativity, Global Lockdown, and the Seductions of Empire," *Radical History Review*, No. 100. 2008, pp. 120–143.

Ahmed, Sara (2004). *The Cultural Politics of Emotion*. New York: Routledge.

Bailey, Alison (2007). "Strategic Ignorance" in *Race & Epistemologies of Ignorance* ed. Nancy Tuana & Shannon Sullivan. Albany: SUNY Press.

Calamur, Krishnadev (2014). "Ferguson Documents: Officer Darren Wilson's Testimony," *NPR* November 25, 2014. Accessed: May 10, 2018. http://www.npr.org/sections/thetwo-way/2014/11/25/366519644/ferguson-docs-officer-darren-wilsons-testimony.

Davis, Angela (2016). *Freedom Is a Constant Struggle: Ferguson, Palestine, and the Foundations of a Movement*. Chicago: Haymarket Books.

Fanon, Frantz (2008). *Black Skin, White Masks*. New York: Grove Press.

Gordon, Lewis (1999). *Bad Faith and Antiblack Racism*. Amherst: Humanity Books.

Gregg, Melissa, Seigworth, Gregory J. (2010). "An Inventory of Shimmers" in *The Affect Theory Reader* ed. Melissa Gregg and Gregory J. Seigworth. Durham and London: Duke University Press.

"Guiding Principles," *Black Lives Matter*. Accessed: July 14, 2016. http://blacklivesmatter.com/guiding-principles/

Knowles, Caroline (2010). "Theorising Race and Ethnicity: Contemporary Paradigms and Perspectives," in *The SAGE Handbook of Race and Ethnic Studies*, ed. Patricia Hill Collins & John Solomos. London: SAGE Publications.

Lugones, María (1987). "Playfulness, 'World'-Travelling, and Loving Perception," *Hypatia* Vol. 2. No. 2. 1987, pp. 3–19.

Mahmood, Saba (2005). *Politics of Piety: The Islamic Revival and the Feminist Subject*. Princeton and Oxford: Princeton University Press.

Maldonado-Torres, Nelson (2007). "On the Coloniality of Being: Contributions to the development of a concept," *Cultural Studies* Vol. 21. No. 2/3. 2007, pp. 240–270.

Merleau-Ponty, Maurice (1962). *Phenomenology of Perception*. New York: Humanities Press.

Mills, Charles (2007). "White Ignorance," *Race and Epistemologies of Ignorance*, ed. Shannon Sullivan and Nancy Tuana. Albany: SUNY Press.

_____ (1997). *The Racial Contract*. Ithaca and London: Cornell University Press.

Myers, Christopher (2013). "Young Dreamers," *The Horn Book*, August 6, 2013. Accessed: July 21, 2016. http://www.hbook.com/2013/08/opinion/young-dreamers/.

Ortega, Mariana (2006). "Being Lovingly, Knowingly Ignorant" *Hypatia* Vol. 21. No. 3. 2006, pp. 56–74.

Protevi, John (2009). *Political Affect: Connecting the Social and the Somatic*. Minneapolis and London: University of Minnesota Press.

Stanko, Elizabeth (1990). *Everyday Violence: How Women and Men Experience Sexual and Physical Danger*. London: Pandora.

Sullivan, Shannon (2006). *Revealing Whiteness: The Unconscious Habits of Racial Privilege* Bloomington: Indiana University Press.

Townley, Cynthia (2006). "Toward a Revaluation of Ignorance," *Hypatia* Vol. 21. No. 3. 2006, pp. 37–55.

"White Like Me" (2008) *The New Adventures of Old Christine*. CBS. Kari's Logo Here & Warning Bros. Television, Los Angeles. 8 Oct. 2008.

Yancy, George (2012). *Look, a White!* Philadelphia: Temple University Press.

_____ (2008a). *Black Bodies, White Gazes*. Lanham: Rowman & Littlefield Publishers.

_____ (2008b). "Elevators, Social Spaces, and Racism." *Philosophy & Social Criticism* Vol. 34. No. 8. 2008, pp. 843–876.

Young, Iris Marion (1980). "Throwing Like a Girl: A Phenomenology of Feminine Body Comportment, Motility, and Spatiality" *Human Studies* Vol. 3. No. 2. 1980, pp. 137–156.

İsmail Serin

Transformation of "Theory" in Modern Philosophy: Some Recent Changes

The theoretical positions and conceptual resources in the contemporary investigation of the philosophical problems had close relation with the discussions
around the fundamental theme of subject and/or subjectivity. Various approaches
towards the question of the subject not only emphasize the nuances among the
major tendencies but also lead novel questions. The aim of this paper is to analyse these philosophical tendencies about the questions of subject and to make
clear their role in forming the "theory." It is discussed that the question of the
theory in all contemporary philosophical approaches is not understood without
determining the status of human subjectivity as the basic characterizing element
of the philosophical perspectives. To analyse these perspectives, first of all, it is
necessary to follow the main formulations of subject in the modern philosophy.
Modern formulations, at first sight, seem to be the result of the movement of a
pendulum between society in general and the subject as a person. Starting from
Descartes this movement of pendulum causes an unbearable and unremovable
duality in western thought. For instance, in order to understand the nature of
the subject we are obliged to analyse its body on the one hand, and its thoughts
on the other hand. While the body of the subject remains in the field of the
natural sciences which means the research will be epistemological in character,
its thoughts will be the subject matter of the social sciences which mean it will
be under the impact of the society. As a result the question of subject does not
require only epistemological reflection, but also political approaching, and for
this reason, if we take into consideration the current political composition of the
world, the existence or non-existence of the subject is defined as a problem not
only philosophically, but fundamentally politically. This twofold structure of the
subject will lead various intellectual frameworks that each will in the end turns
into a "theory".

The Rise of the Subject

The theoretical formulation of subject/subjectivity in the modern philosophy is
connected with the development of the modern scientific and rationalist society as
the project of the Enlightenment Age. Many philosophers in this period attended

to the problem of the subject as the problem of grounding their philosophical systems and of attributing specific function to subject for the sake of a more general program. Descartes, is the first philosopher in the seventeenth century presented such a program, regarded subjectivity as the capacity of having an idea about God. Thus his philosophy elaborated on the questions about the reliability of perception, presented in his comprehensive writings on natural philosophy which is based on his foundationalist program. In fact the basic contemporary debates about subjectivity, as Atkins argues, originate from Descartes's problematic description of the status of subject in terms of both natural philosophy and rationalism. By his description of subject he essentially attempted to unite the metaphysical and empirical aspects of the problem of subject. Descartes's characterization of the subject in terms of the matter (body) and thought (mind) was expressive of his dual commitments: science and religion.[1]

The Enlightenment project as the one of the general foundationalist program of the modern philosophy was so presented firstly by Descartes. Then Kant provides the intellectual stand for the scientific outlook which is known to be the most influential expression of this program. It arose in an era of social and political disputes triggered by the religious and class warfare inflamed by the Reformation. Thorough out these social controversies all claims about truth and moral judgments were generally based on religious prejudices and particular political interests without any universal validity claim. However, the foundationalist program, like Descartes's dualistic method, contributed to overcome these difficulties. His success lies in a persuasion of an entire generation of thinker that, by carefully following a prescribed method, it is possible to arrive at truths unspoiled by perspectives and values grounded in particular interests. According to Cartesian method, clear and distinct knowledge may only be achieved if the knower gets rid of all his beliefs deriving from unreliable sources like the dominant convictions among people. This is the method of universal doubt. So, it is no wonder that one of the basic features of the philosophy in the early seventeenth century become the skeptical approach to the problems of the philosophy.

By following this method of universal doubt, it became possible for any thinker to get at least a universally valid knowledge which is founded on the fact of her/his own existence free from the nationality, the gender, the religious faith or the social class. The capacities of the subject are seen enough to decide what is

---

1   Kim Atkins summarizes the process how Descartes's dualism is not only limited in
    philosophy, but affects our all our intellectual outlook (Atkins, 2005: 1–4).

wrong and what is right. The supremacy of the subject clears and disables all the maladies of the past. One thing remains free from doubt: the contents of one's own mind.

The argument for the denial of this position is found in Wittgenstein's work, *Philosophical Investigations* and is concerned with what would have to be the case for us to possess the whole range of mental concepts in the absence of other people and relationship. The relevance of Wittgenstein's point to the very heart of political philosophy, follows from the claim that it is not possible to derive a set of values about human flourishing, or the nature of human needs and desires, without looking at the social context which makes that account of flourishing or needs intelligible and provides a justification for it.

Descartes believed that, by depending on the truth of the existence of the human mind we may establish a body of truths that would be forever immune to doubt. In this way, all human knowledge gains an absolutely secure foundation (hence "foundationalism"). Scepticism was defeated. Through Descartes's method the knower obviously distinguishes "objective" truth from "subjective" belief.

Though the whole story is long and complex, its solution to the problem of scepticism is clear and distinct. The Cartesian philosophy had become the basis for the dominant conviction of the majority principle that governs the most western European democracies. This majority principle was known best by being scientific and universalist. In its own self-understanding, its knowledge was simply objective as such. It was not an ordinary view among other views. It was and is still a view-from-nowhere. All other cultural positions (those of non-western countries as well as those of underdeveloped social classes within western societies) were more or less assumed to be hopelessly sunk in pre-scientific prejudices and negligible interests.

While the basis of this claim was buttressed by the Cartesian method, especially its application in nature generated a tool that we now called scientific method. This method creates not only objective knowledge which is the sole judge but makes the past immature at best. Since no tradition is scientific in nature, they all devoid of being objective, and have an unjustified power on their members. Traditional social orders from this aspect seem to be replaced without further ado by a better and more developed one in which all relations and institutions are rationally established. Unlike pre-modern times public sphere does not respect the past just for the sake of their historical values. Cartesian dichotomy draws a line between tradition which is the content of culture and public sphere which is established by the bourgeoisie completely. This means a new war between the past and the present.

As a product of such setting the boundaries of the public sphere, the explicit distinction between "state" and "society" was made. It seems that it was Hegel who first systematically developed the distinction between "civil society" and the "state". In Hegel's account the two spheres are independent but it is the state that is the highest form of human association. But Hegel attempts to link specific forms of society and the different accounts of nature of the self and its ends together into some metaphysical theory which saw them as progressing towards more and more adequate forms of human fulfilment in world history. The rejection of such a meta-narrative of legitimation defines the other standpoint of postmodernism. However, it does agree with Hegel that social meanings are historical, they change over time and present meanings have to be understood in terms of their historical development. This means that there cannot be a universal political philosophy, so there cannot be a transhistorical one. What counts as the relevant reasons for action depends not upon some essentialist or trans-cultural or trans-historical theory but upon the contingent circumstances of particular cultures.

The Fall of the Subject

This approach rethinks the nature of political philosophy. It interprets the values, principles and reasons which play a critical role for human actions. According to them no one can exist in a culture-free realm, thus it is highly reasonable to reject the validity of universal principles, and to defend a new kind of political philosophy in which relativism, diversity, difference and plurality are the key concepts. For instance, traditional class politics is replaced by the identity politics.

In such a case it seems that there is no possible mediation between universality and particularity. But Ernesto Laclau claimed, "the assertion of pure particularism, independent of any appeal to a universality, is a self-defeating enterprise" (Laclau, 1992: 87). Since, if we take particularism as the only valid principle or the only accepted normative principle, it confronts us with an unsolvable paradox. We can defend the right of sexual, racial, and national minorities in the name of particularism, but we have to accept also the rights to self-determination of all kinds of reactionary groups involved in antisocial practices (Laclau, 1992: 87). Laclau argues, in fact there is no particularism that does not appeal to more general principles in the construction of its own identity. These principles may be progressive such as the right of peoples to self-determination or may be reactionary such as social Darwinism but they are always there, and for essential reason (Laclau, 1992: 88).

The assertion of particularism, independent of any appeal to a universality, represents also the first steps toward a reconstructing of political analysis in accordance with the pluralistic principles of civic rationality. The pluralities of interpretation and representation in politics offers a variety of new perspectives and to look forward to the postmodern social world and it presumes the death of the foundational approach to political analysis. The role of formal political institutions as well as the public actions of those has become part of the manifestation of the crisis of the political.

This crisis in the political is one dimension of a more general sense of disintegration in the human sciences. A central aspect of this disintegration is the intellectual fragmentation that is a consequence of modernist disciplinary specialisation. This has led not only a revival of interest in inter- and cross-disciplinary work, but also to a recognition of the importance of "boundary work" in the production of knowledge. By the abounding scepticsm towards grand narratives, here one may consider Lyotard's short but influential work *The Postmodern Condition*, (Lyotard, 1984) and by the rise of unfoundationalist stance towards both political and social theory[2] the crisis of the humanities in its disintegration has led to the rise of interests in cultural studies.

Stuart Hall explains, in his article, the appearance of cultural studies and its project from the point of view of the United Kingdom and from his own experience at the Center for Cultural Studies in Birmingham. The important point is that he does not take the problem of the humanities and social technology within the terms of its disintegration and of crisis in the humanities. He thinks, although cultural studies in Britain emerged from a *crisis* in the humanities, the disintegration of humanities is not the result of the cultural studies, but social conditions. In fact he does not think that there is such disintegration. The self-presentation of the humanities as an ongoing, integral, integrated exercise brings to this idea of disintegration. He says that the humanities have never been or can no longer be that integral formation (Hall, 1990: 12).

For Stuart Hall, cultural studies in Britain begin with the attempt to understand the nature of social and cultural change in Britain after the Second World War. Since the Left's critique of capitalism no longer provided the basis for an adequate analysis of post-war conditions. Capitalism appeared to have leapt to a new level of development, and the Left was faced with the need to reinvent itself

---

2   In his "Postmodernist Bourgeois Liberalism" Rorty discusses two camps quarrelling on the nature of the community. Kantians, according to him, believes in "intrinsic human dignity," Hegelians on the other hand argues that "there is no human dignity that is not derivative from the dignity of some specific community" (Rorty, 1983: 583).

and its vision of politics. By the expansion of consumerism, capitalism filled the culture with new devices and entertainments. As the founders of cultural studies said, culture *mattered* and the Left needed to recognize this phenomenon and organize work around it. This new direction formed the task of cultural studies. Stuart Hall defines this task is "to provide ways of thinking, strategies for survival, and recourse to all those who are now in economic, political, and cultural terms excluded from anything that could be called access to the national culture of the national community" (Hall, 1990: 22).

The rise of cultural studies has led to new theoretical and methodological directions, such as critical analysis of race and gender, structualist procedures for the study of ideology and media, and ethnographic procedures for the study of media audience. Thus, cultural studies seemed as the studies of theories of cultural pluralism included not only ethnic diversity, but also multiculturalism, identity politics, the politics of difference.

Multiculturalism is the application of the principle of cultural pluralism as proper to the liberal democratic political tradition and it is a means of rethinking post-war policies towards cultural minorities. Multiculturalism as an affirmation of such a pluralism does not trouble most of us, but it troubles as the form of ethnocentrism (Eurocentricism), the literary canon, and the cultural politics of difference.

One of the critics of multiculturalism is made by Stanley Fish. He argues that in its strong version the multiculturalism takes difference as a general principle, but not as any *particular* difference (Fish, 1997: 384). Thus, this multiculturalism cannot allow full realizing the imperatives of particular difference in a political program. In the other words, such multiculturalism as Fish called strong multiculturalism honors diversity in general, but cannot honor a particular instance of diversity. For example, Fish tells, someone may find something of value in rap music and patronize soul-food restaurants, but s/he will be uneasy about affirmative action and downright hostile to an afrocentrist cirriculum (Fish, 1997: 378). Fish called this kind of multiculturalism not as strong multiculturalism, but *boutique multiculturalism* (Fish, 1997: 384).

Žižek underlines a new current in racism: postmodern racism (Žižek, 1997: 37) with a distance "it respects the Other's identity, conceiving the Other as a self-enclosed 'authentic' community towards which he maintains a distance rendered possible by his privileged universal position"(Žižek, 1997: 44). Žižek sees multiculturalism as the ideal form of ideology of global capitalism, which involves *colonization without the colonizing* Nation-State metropole and involves patronizing Eurocentrist distance and/or respect for local cultures without roots in one's own particular culture (Žižek, 1997: 44). Žižek summarizes the historical generation of the global capitalism at three stages. At the first stage, there is capitalism within the confines of a Nation-State, with the accompanying international trade; at the second, in the relationship of colonization, the colonizing country subordinates and exploits (economically, politically, culturally) the colonized country; at the final stage of this process, the colonizing power is no longer a Nation-State but directly the global company. This is the today's global capitalism as the paradox of colonization in which there are only colonies, no colonizing countries (Žižek, 1997: 44). According to Žižek, this process shows that in the long term, "we shall all not only wear Banana Republic shirts but also live in banana republics."

In the light of the new directions provided by such a global capitalism and cultural studies, Stuart Hall, under the influence of Louis Althusser's and the French Marxists' writings, re-evaluated the human condition within actuality. He argued that people imagine human actions to be free, or at least self-chosen, when in reality people spend life within the limits of cultural frameworks and structured social roles and identities.

This means that the line between the *private* and the *public*, or, personal/individual and social is artificial. If so, this also implies the achievement of modernity which social theory has suggested, is to erase particularity and create a universality: to create an identity, it might be called, which turns on no particular save that of the nation-state whose nationality, as its citizens, we share, and turns on no properties beyond those we are given by law. This is not to say that we are not individuated. The state requires us to be. But the individuation it demands says nothing about who we are as persons or in society. It serves merely to identify our public status as private citizens of the state. If we retain anything of a more particular kind that is also public, it is our position in the market.

Such position of individual in the public brings to the problem for the legitimation of the methods used by the social research, and the problem of the distinction between the individual opinion and the public opinion for the empirical social research. Since, in the case of individuals limited with cultural frameworks and structured with social roles and identities, not the individual but the society has all the makings of opinions in circulation. But as one can argue convincingly that individual opinion, which is defined traditionally as the content of a person's consciousness, without any judgements about its truth or untruth, does not depend only on culturally and socially structured identity, but also internal psychological structure of the person. Now, a problem for the empirical social research arises on the basis of the question of how the objective facts of the society are to be researched without eliminating the subjective impulse of the individual. Adorno, at this point reminds us that

[t]radition is opposed to rationality, even though the one took shape in the other. Its medium is not consciousness but the pregiven, unreflected and binding existence of social forms — the actuality of the past; unintentionally this notion of binding existence was transmitted to the intellectual/spiritual sphere. Tradition in the strict sense is incompatible with bourgeois society (Adorno, 1992: 75).

If modern society is hostile to the tradition in principle, then it would be useless to conduct empirical studies on society as a whole or on individuals as a person.

These problems related with the object and technique of the empirical social research shows that the real problem is the public opinion. In the empirical social research there is approached to the concept of the public opinion as the essence of all individual opinions. This concept of public opinion presupposes a social organisation or group the members of which have to have more or less common experience (or discursively achieved consensus). But this leads to the existence of opinion-forming groups and atomistic conception of public opinion. Such a notion of public opinion does not represent merely a collection of individual opinions, but contains a blanket collective component. It is impossible to determine this component by any scientific measurement. But in the empirical research of opinion, only individual opinions can be counted and measured. The public opinion does not give an adequate of the facts and it is still under the influence of the interrelation between institutional intellectual forces and individuals, between one individual and another.

Pierre Bourdieu, by his analysis of the functions of opinion polls, goes further and says that public opinion does not exist. His analysis starts with calling into question the three postulates of the opinion polls: First postulate is that, "everyone can have an opinion", in the other words; producing an opinion is something available to all. For him this, in fact, implies only probability, probability of having an opinion. The non-responses, or 'don't knows', or 'no answer' is ignored in this postulate. The second postulate is that, "all opinions have equal value". This is the dream of liberal ideologies. As Bourdieu pointed out, opinions cannot have the same strength and the cumulation of such opinions leads to the meaningless artefacts. The third postulate is that, "there is a concensus on what the problems are, in the other words; there is agreement on the questions that are worth asking."

If everyone doesn't have opinions having the same strength, and having opinion implies only a probability, then there cannot be any way to determine any concensus or agreement on what the problems are. All these mean that, as Bourdieu said, there is no something called public opinion in the sense of the purely arithmetical total of individual opinions (Bourdieu, 1993: 150).

If the opinion poll is an instrument of political action, what the effect produced by this kind of poll will not reflect an objective concensus about policy
based on the public opinion. This means that concensus effect can be produced
(Bourdieu, 1993: 151). Instead of public opinion, as Bourdieu says, there is mobilized opinion, formulated opinion by pressure groups mobilized around a system
of explicitly formulated interests (Bourdieu, 1993: 157).

Derrida defines such formulation of public interests, and its artificiality as
deconstruction of actuality. Unlike Bourdieu, Derrida does *not* see the artificiality *only* in the meaning of questions or problems, but also in determining
what the problems are there. For Derrida what is important is not only to know
the artificiality of actuality, the actuality is indeed made, or produced. But what
more necessary is to know the time of public act is produced artificially, and recognize what the actuality is made of, and by which producers and instruments
the actuality is produced (Derrida, 1994: 28).

According to Derrida, the time of a public act in its actualization is calculated and constrained, formatted and initialised by the organisation of media
(Derrida, 1994: 28). Therefore, as he remarked, anyone who wants to think their
present is bound to pay heed to a public space and bound to a political present which is constantly changing in form and content as a result of the "tele-
technology" of what is confusedly called news, information or communication
(Derrida, 1994: 28).

Coda

As a result of this tele-technology, the printing press, the computer, and television are no longer simply machines which transmit information, but create
entities through which reality is reorganised in one way or another way. Through
these media figures, we do not see the reality as it is. The main problem is not
whether such tele-technology, or media figures determine the present, but
rather, what the effects of such media as technical carriers of political forces are.
In fact, to understand these effects in terms of a direct cause and effect, if we take
into consideration the ongoing debates in the world arena, is no longer possible.
These effects are mediated by social, economic and cultural factors. Tradition
transforms into a new reality in which it seems to remain unchanged, but in fact
it has changed deeply.

The new directions provided by global capitalism emerged the new structures
of power (the global media power as servant of global capital markets), power
relationship, and the new forms of organisations which are best seen in the relationship between state-university-science-technology-industry. Technology is

no longer only the application of science, but it became a method wholly subservient to military and civic needs which are themselves inventions. Universities became projects producing institutions for the global companies in order to increase their profit.

The rise of cultural studies as affirmation of a global culture of multiplicity and difference has led to an uncritical celebration of culture. The rise of the global media power as servant of global capital markets has led to people to a life packaged with the indeterminate contents. It cannot be ignored that in promoting cultural pluralities the role of the State which is directed, in terms of its government, civil service, armed forces and other organisations, by the global market enterprises was increased, and the goal of equality as the basic ideal of liberal democracies was not achieved by the simple recognition of cultural difference. What needed is, as Honneth argues, "(...) a minimal concept of "community" that is already formulated in such a way as to contain the presupposition of human self-realization that is linked to the existence of a common way of life" (Honneth, 2007: 255).

In this paper we tried to argue that the motive that creates vital discussions about role of theory in modern philosophy is mostly depends on Cartesian dichotomies. This problematic, in our case, determines both the future of the society and the past of the individual. As Honneth puts:

> (..) the battle initiated by the bourgeoisie on the threshold of modernity against the nobility's feudal conception of honor was not only a collective attempt to establish new principles of value, but also the opening move in a confrontation over the status of such principles in general. For the first time, doubts were raised as to whether a person's social standing ought to be measured by the previously established value of qualities typifyingly attributed to entire groups of people. Now, the individual as a distinct biographical figure began to enter the disputed field where social esteem is allocated (Honneth, 2007: 260).

Our current task is still critical but neither in Kantian nor Hegelian sense. It is rather in-between position.

References

Adorno, T. W. (1992). On Tradition. *Telos*, (94), 75–82. https://doi.org/10.3817/1293094075

Atkins, K. (Ed.). (2005). Introduction. In *Self and Subjectivity* (pp. 1–4). Oxford, UK: Blackwell Publishing Ltd. https://doi.org/10.1002/9780470774847.ch

Bourdieu, P. (1993). Public Opinion does not Exist. In R. Nice (Trans.), *Sociology in Question* (pp. 149–157). London: Sage Publications.

Derrida, J. (1994). The deconstruction of actuality. *Radical Philosophy*, (68), 28–41.

Fish, S. (1997). Boutique Multiculturalism, or Why Liberals Are Incapable of Thinking about Hate Speech. *Critical Inquiry*, *23*(2), 378–395. https://doi.org/10.1086/448833

Hall, S. (1990). The Emergence of Cultural Studies and the Crisis of the Humanities. *October*, *53*, 11–23. https://doi.org/10.2307/778912

Honneth, A. (2007). Post-traditional Communities: A Conceptual Proposal. In J. Ganahl (Trans.), *Disrespect : the normative foundations of critical theory* (pp. 254–262). Cambridge: Polity Press.

Laclau, E. (1992). Universalism, Particularism, and the Question of Identity. *October*, *61*, 83. https://doi.org/10.2307/778788

Lyotard, J.-F. (1984). *The postmodern condition : a report on knowledge*. (G. Bennington & B. Massumi, Trans.). Minneapolis: University of Minnesota Press.

Rorty, R. (1983). Postmodernist Bourgeois Liberalism. *The Journal of Philosophy*, *80*(10), 583–589. https://doi.org/10.2307/2026153

Žižek, S. (1997). Multiculturalism, or, the cultural logic of multinational capitalism. *New Left Review*, (225), 28–51. https://doi.org/10.1111/j.1467-8330.1993.tb00220.x

Mehmet Şiray

The Aesthetic Movement of Politics in Jacques Rancière's Political Theory

1 Introduction

Jacques Rancière, one of the most prominent French philosophers of our times, claims that aesthetics is political in the sense that art practices intervene with "the distribution of the sensible" (*le partage du sensible*) which is defined as the existence of common with its respective parts and positions within it while politics also has an aesthetic of its own by creating stages. In this context, art and politics are not mutually exclusive realities; both are realities that depend on the distribution of the sensible. The purpose of the chapter is to understand politics, which finds its center in the visibility of politics depending on that which is aesthetical, and argue that considering the aesthetics of the political is an inevitable requisite of comprehending politics. Politics, in the broadest sense, unites or materializes practices of living, thinking and doing as a whole through the re-initiation and regulation of the mechanisms of visibility. Aesthetics, here, does not refer to beauty in the first instance, but it is a form of framing spaces and times, of the visible and the invisible, of speech and noise, as a regime of what is visible and audible. Politics revolves around what is seen and what can be said about it, around the properties of spaces and the possibilities of time. Political actions are ways of doing and making, which intervene in the general distribution of ways of doing and making as well as in the relationships they maintain to the modes of being and forms of visibility.

Rancière aims to develop a concept of politics that is detached from the *polis* described as the organization of powers and the legitimation of the distribution of places and roles, and that he therefore has to rethink the setting of political action, which becomes the stage, a stage which can be located anywhere, not necessarily in central state (or *polis*) institutions. He proposes another term "politics" that stands against such arrangements, and calls the position of those who have no part. The chapter alleges that the encounter between aesthetics and politics also requires a critical examination of how the conditions of spectatorship occurs and transforms the spectacle. Claiming that politics depends on the conditions of visibility means that aesthetics of the political exist, however politics, first and foremost, understood as the act of politics cannot wholly be defined by police since it points at new forms of life through displaying disagreement.

While asserting that politics emerged as an objection to the distribution of the sensible, the chapter focuses that political analysis is only possible by elucidating the aesthetics of the political. The chapter aims at defining politics as a fictive dimension, a stage, which must be understood as a reconfiguration of perception and signification. This approach allows for the study to analyze politics in a larger context that politics implies that its function has the power to understand sovereignty, political subjectivation and the production of political space.

In the first section, I will discuss the relationship between politics and philosophy. In the following section, I will focus on three different forms of political actions and the modern form of politics. In this context, I will first examine Rancière's approach to concepts of "dissensus", "consensus", "politics", "political", "equality", "subjectification" and "democracy". Then, I will elaborate on the relationship between politics and aesthetics through which I will describe the dominant forms of political staging. In the final section, I will underline that Rancière attempts to guide us to the idea of disagreement, which is intrinsic to politics, and reaches this conclusion via the concepts of equality and emancipation, which are central to rethinking politics.

2 The Relationship between Politics and Philosophy: Philosophy of Politics or Politics of Philosophers?

For Jacques Rancière, the question of when political philosophy became one of the subjects of philosophy is a critical one. According to him Plato, along with Socrates, is the first to practice the "art of politics". In the foreword of *La Mésentente: Politique et Philosophy*, Rancière quoting Aristotle emphasizes that the question we tend to forget is "equality or inequality of what sort of thing?" and that "political philosophy" entered philosophy with this question (Rancière, 1995/1999: 7). From Rancière's perspective, Socrates in his search for the truth rendered politics essential to philosophy, and favoured the "politics of philosophers" over the "politics of politicians" (Rancière, 1995/1999: 9). Rancière's assessment moves in this direction: The correlation between the transformation of politics and the simultaneous occurrence of political philosophy as an essential component of philosophy is a particularly challenging philosophical argument to prove (Rancière, 1995/1999: 9). According to Rancière, one of the fundamental difficulties of practicing philosophy, and questioning the nature of philosophy lies in discovering what is intrinsic to philosophy; this difficulty could also be mentioned for philosophy's relationship with other fields that seem essential to philosophy. In this regard, the relation of philosophy to its fields; for example, it becomes necessary to think the conditions of the encounter of politics and philosophy, and maybe as a result leading the way to philosophy taking politics adjective. Thinking contrarily, to position philosophy as a manifestation of a particular ideology and/or politics would reproduce the *aporia* between philosophy and politics. If we regard the problem from the viewpoint of the present, especially the emphasis put on the praxis philosophy from Marx to the present, the criticism that philosophy is nothing more than a specialized politics practiced in a particular way, and in this regard, the birth of a new political philosophy that would propose solutions to *aporias* of both politics and philosophy, would revive the relationship between philosophy and politics.

From Rancière's viewpoint, the periodic clash between politics and philosophy on the subject of equality, in other words philosophy's attempt to offer answers to the question of how to distribute possessions on different levels, also defines how philosophy became political. This relationship without a doubt is an activity with equality as its principle; questions Rancière raises such as "When is there and when is there not equality in things between who and who else?", "What are these "things" and who are these figures?", and ultimately "How does equality come to consist of equality and inequality?" urge us to rethink the relationship between politics and philosophy in terms of the principle of equality (Rancière, 1995/1999: 9–14).

Rancière's second important assessment could be stated as follows: in the encounter between philosophy and politics, the occurrence of disagreement (*dissensus*) is a requisite for the generation of intellectual activity. Following Rancière, disagreement should not be considered merely a misunderstanding, incomprehension, or confusion, an uncertainty about words. Rancière defines all arrangements from Plato to the present that we will call political philosophy, as strategies of disagreement. Rancière attempts to reveal something that could simply be considered politics by detaching politics from the term *polis*. While the term *polis* derives from the same root as politics, it implies the existence of people living together in a certain order; in this context, *polis* is the actions of people who attempt to resolve disagreements on the basis of rationality. Rancière does not use the term *polis* in the Althusserian sense, which is the ideological apparatus of the state. *Polis* is the name of the order that regulates positions and affairs, defines social relations signifying who has and who doesn't have a part in the partition. He calls another presence that stands against such arrangements, and calls the position of those who have no part, the politics. *Polis* depends on the "principle of equality", in a sense social order means an organizational schema where equality is operated. Rancière calls the equality that evokes a rather "empty equality and freedom", used in the sense of emancipation that is at the centre of the practices we call the state, the "logic of equality". The more politics can move outside of the logic of equality and *polis*, the more space of freedom and move-ment it will have for itself. In this regard, we have to assert that the political renders itself effectively through the principle of equality, and it should also be noted that politics could not be considered as absolutely apart from the order of police, because nothing is political in itself. Political philosophy that establishes the state and the society in opposition assume a certain combination of *polis* and politics. By showing whether or not the orders that depend on the logic of equality are political, Rancière tries to demonstrate how they operate the prin-ciple of equality in the course of this evolving issue.

The role the concept of subjectification plays in this process is crucial in terms of the conditions that politics come to exist. According to Rancière, subjectification is the name for the reshaping of a field of experience that has not been previously specified or identified. In this context, subjectification is natu-rally against the logic of *polis*, and being so bears a potential to reveal a series of that which is unexpressed. Rancière states that during this process idiosyncratic subject positions such as "proletariat", "woman", "queer", "worker", "student", and "poor" may rise and have already arisen. According to Rancière, these names represent those who are the uncounted or the speechless of the community, and they are the elements of a subjectification process that reveals "a wrong" (Rancière, 1995/1999: 36). The process of occurrence and subjectification of pol-itics comes to life with the emergence of thoughts that depend on the principle of equality, and the expression of the principle of equality gives rise to a "universal polemic", and the birth of an alternate world to the one in which those receive the lion's share of the social partition (Rancière, 1995/1999: 62–63). Political subjectification reveals the wrong and the problems within the *polis* order with the idea of a common world and community, leading to new relationships and bonds between people.

Rancière mentions that in the relationship between philosophy and poli-tics, politics takes precedence over philosophy because politics always refers to a factual reality. Socrates assumes that he practices "the truest" politics and introduces himself to his followers as such, assigning one of philosophy's self-ap-pointed values from the very beginning. Political philosophy that reflects the philosopher's (biased) opinion on democracy takes its place in the philosophical scene as the "politics of philosophers" (Rancière, 1995/1999: 62–63). In Plato's state, as an authority that determines and distributes the parts of those "who don't have any part", philosophy shall rectify all the dysfunctional elements of the city, and bring unity to it. Rancière places the beginnings of political philosophy right when he starts mentioning the politics of the philosophers, and underlines that philosophy defines itself as politics by promising to solve inequality. In this context, political philosophy shapes a set of notions creating lines of consensus for disagreement, and calls it philosophy of politics. According to Rancière, philosophy's attempt to distance itself from disagreement through rationality is philosophy's attempt to define its essence, that which is intrinsic to philosophy. This is what renders philosophy political; philosophy attains this position by the reduction of disagreement, which is fundamentally intrinsic to politics.

3 Three Stages of Politics: Archipolitics, Parapolitics and Metapolitics

Rancière calls three major stages of political philosophy archipolitics, parapolitics and metapolitics. Rancière establishes Plato put forth in *Republic* that The State as a structure defines and distributes of what is common by law, distributes the good and those who have a lesser part, organizes education and the division of labor, and determines moral responsibilities and roles, and as such is itself defined as archipolitics. According to Rancière, *Republic* stages a common life (*ethos*) where the good take over and oppression emerges, social law mediates the individual and that which is common is very *polis* itself. In the consensus, the existence of those without the right of speech is acknowledged yet it is presumed that they cannot be included in the social life. Socrates' demonstration in *Meno* that the slave is smart enough to solve a mathematical puzzle yet lacks the intelligence to be a part of society (and therefore the government) could stand as a clear example. The most substantial complication for Plato is that those without the power of speech aspire for public office, and that people desire to undertake different tasks. The main reason why democracy fails to function is that it creates this complication. Plato's *Republic* confirms a social body in which one cannot be a shoemaker and a painter at the same time; according to him everybody is supposed to do whatever their reason for being is (Rancière, 1983/2003: 4). With the definition of state being that which distinguishes useful from harmful, Plato assumes an order that aims for the common good. According to Rancière, one of the most important elements of what defines the public (*demos*) from past to the present that leads to the denial of politics is the wealthy classes tendency to think that those who do not have a part in the common wealth don't exist.

As Rancière claims, Aristotle operates the logic of equality bringing forth the law for common life to be established just like Plato does. Parapolitics is an act of mediation that brings together the best aspects of all constitutional forms (oligarchy, democracy and timocracy). In the first chapter of *Politics*, Aristotle states that one of the requirements of establishing political order is that people with the power of speech be able to distinguish useful from harmful. According to

Aristotle, the good and the just are related in essence. Similarly to Plato, Aristotle says that in a political order that would be expressed with reason, justice is the only virtue to distinguish useful from harmful. In a sense Aristotle, by placing the public's (*demos*) freedom against the virtue of the wealthy and noble (oligarchy of the wealthy, democracy of the people, and aristocracy of the virtuous), tries to solve and mediate these differences. It seems to me that Rancière reveals that Aristotle and Plato have the struggle between the rich and the poor at the core of their political philosophies. This struggle is exactly what constitutes politics itself; politics is the constitution of the poor (as a *demos*) as an entity. Politics always indicates a struggle that rises on these grounds; yet we may consider politics as a place where classes may know themselves differently from what they are.

Parapolitics is another archetype of the "politics of philosophers" aiming for the common good and where those who have no right to govern are excluded while the rest are mediated with the state. Thomas Hobbes refines Aristotle's constitutional forms through the relations between the state and individual, turning the social contract into a political form. As in the previous ways of practicing politics, those who have no part in the common wealth (public, masses, crowds, communities that don't tend to comply) are excluded from the equation of equality. In Rancière's final analysis, even though the mode of politics changed with Hobbes the logic of equality remains the same, and thus parapolitics acquires a modern appearance.

Metapolitics undertakes the task of ending earlier forms of politics and furthermore exposes the failure of these politics. This new political movement uses a terminology containing terms like "social", "social problems", "social class" and "real social movement" and reconstructs philosophy that depends on action (*praxis*) in order to expose the failure of prior political forms (Rancière, 1995/1999: 82). Rancière states that Marx clearly expressed the legislative formulation of metapolitical interpretation in *On The Jewish Question*. Marx argues that politics is a fabrication about a reality called the society; according to him, if actualized, the act of production and class struggle movements would become the true movement to chase away and destroy the aspects of political citizenship in favour of working people (Rancière, 1995/1999: 82).

Rancière states Marx places those who have not part into a new partition, and that the basis of this distribution is a subjectification that depends on class struggle. Thus Marx placed a metapolitical understanding that surpassed the ways of practicing politics before him. Rancière's ideological analysis should be read in this manner; ideology, the truth as a name for the wrongness of other political stances, let's call this the real truth of class struggle, reveals the other. At this stage, Rancière thinks that Marx has announced the end of politics but politics was reconstructed through its negation. Rancière calls the period after Marx that universalizes that which is social and turns the logic of equality into slogan, the age of sociology. For Rancière, the age of democracy in which political subjects achieve operability through a social body is nothing more than singing praises to the actualization of the so-called government of enlightened individuals aiming for the common good. Here Rancière focuses on the story of the alteration of the idea of transformative subject (*proletariat*), that Marx placed in the centre of social dynamics, into a political body (*subjectification*) that reveals itself as the *polis* through European democracy. For Rancière rebirth of politics through its negation (or from its ashes) has lead to emergence a new political form called the parliamentary democracy. Rancière would call this new form of democracy the "democracy of consensus" in "post-democracy" era. Rancière declares that the latest political attempt in today's world where inequality is sought to be produced with the promise of equality is the consensus democracy. According to him both liberals and socialists agree that this dialect of democracy fails to live up to its promise of democratization; besides, the age of democracy where the struggle between those who have no part ("the mutes" as Rancière calls them) and the other sections of the society has disappeared, has turned into an image which renders the invisible visible for everybody. According to Rancière, the political philosophy still in this day, views the idea of political community through possible results of the aesthetic revolution Kant set forth. Freedom and equality scenarios that has shaped with the Kantian idea of enlightenment, is based on having reason emerging from the *free-play* of this imagery, and "equality" of sensibility (Rancière, 2010: 81).

According to Rancière, ideals of egalitarian society contain a discourse that is inherently foreign to it's own existence or provides an alternative or contesting discourse, and because they base the equality of the given collective reason on a non-egalitarian (not actual) ideal of society, are stuck on an idea of consensus rather than that of disagreement. In the final analysis, Rancière states especially the European democracy fails to achieve even its own ideals; the post-democracy that could be viewed as the continuation of metapolitics, has drifted from the idea of a democracy that would have formed around "emancipation" and "criticism". The possibility of politics has vanished. One the most fundamental drives behind Rancière's effort to define the three stages of political philosophy that depends on a principle of equality is his attempt to detach politics from the political as state of living together. Another one is that he avoids presenting the concept of democracy as an already defined form of governance. According to Rancière politics, even though it is associated with forms of political dominance, cannot be reduced to a mere art of governing the masses; politics is a human action based on disagreement (Rancière, 1992/1995: 11).

Rancière asserts that the notion of politics is different from the notion of political power, defining politics in an activity of subjectification detaches it from the political. What is political is a process that can be defined with the polis process, in other words organizing and regulating the affairs of people living together, but it is also a process that counts and regulates the uncounted. But according to Rancière, politics is rather the practices of liberation that operates by the principle that anyone is equal to anyone else, and attempts to affirm this principle. Thus what initiates the equality principle is the inequality itself. That which is political (notion of social life) always departs from an assumption of an equality originating from inequality. Rancière in various contexts at school, at work and mainly at the state explains assembling political subjects he calls rationalization process in this way. For example, Jacotot in *The Ignorant Schoolmaster* shows us that the hierarchal arrangement between the student and the teacher, on which the educational system depends, is this very rationalization process itself (Rancière, 1987/1991: 5–6).

We observe that Rancière employs the concepts of politics and democracy synonymously in some of his passages; according to him neither politics nor a form of political life is a type of dominance (Hewlett, 2007: 113). We can maintain Rancière draws this parallelism in order to give voice to the criticisms towards the limited form of democracy, and through the possibility for the occurrence of a radical liberation. In this context, I have to add that Rancière's efforts to redefine politics, attempts to bring a breath of fresh air to those subjects who desire to get away from the desperate European democracy's view of democracy that has mediated with global economy.

4 Conclusion

According to Rancière, art is political in the broadest sense only while it remains as an opportunity to unite or materialize practices of living, thinking and doing as a whole through the re-initiation and regulation of the mechanisms of perception and sense. Based on this definition, politics too should be arranged as politics of a place, of people that cluster around certain commonalities and this sense of commonality should be identified as a determination of this type of experience. As stated above politics is not about using a power (government) or the struggle for such power; politics is a new staging and rearrangement of each and every element of this stage. As a claim for a common world, politics occurs through a staging (*mis en scène*) that brings community and non-community together. "The distribution of the sensible" expression Rancière frequently utters, reminds us that the relationship between politics, as the distribution or the staging of the sensible, and aesthetics is essential. Democracy and theatre, which witnessed the birth of politics, are intertwined as the two heterogeneous forms of the distribution of the sensible, in Ancient Greece. Maybe that is why both are forced to retreat from the common life, because the distribution of the sensible not only underlines the grounds of commonality but allocates, distributes those who are excluded (Rancière, 1992/1994:32).

Rancière in his "Ten Theses on Politics" while stating that politics emerged as an objection to the distribution of the sensible argues that political analysis is only possible by elucidating the aesthetics of politics, and only thus will it be possible to mention a radical democracy. From Rancière's perspective, the problem is to compare the positions of the subjects of the common life, and for this the aesthetics of which that is political must be accounted for, from the very beginning. In this respect, to reveal the radical dissimilarity of politics, what is required is not a regime of historical verification or a discourse of truth but grounds on which history can mediate with its own story. Because the relationship of politics and aesthetics depends on the distribution between that which is visible and invisible, audible and inaudible, we can declare aesthetics of politics as the *topos* where this disagreement takes place. Therefore the relationship between aesthetics and politics is between aesthetics of politics as the loss of appearance and politics as the liberation of appearance. For that which is political to be aesthetical means that which is political turning into spectacle and transforming it into a form of discourse.

References

Hewlett, Nick (2007). *Badiou, Balibar, Rancière: Rethinking Emancipation.* London, New York: Continuum.

Rancière, Jacques (1999). *Dis-aggrement: Politics and Philosophy.* (Juli Rose, Trans.) Minneapolis, London: University of Minnesota Press (Original work published 1995).

Rancière, Jacques (1983). *The Philosopher and His Poor.* (John Drury, Corinne Oster and Andrew Parker, Trans.) Minneapolis, Durham, London: Duke University Press (Original work published 2003).

Rancière, Jacques (2010). *Dissensus: On Politics and Aesthetics.* (Steven Corcoran, Trans.) Londra, New York: Continuum.

Rancière, Jacques (1991). *The Ignorant School Master.* (Kristin Rose, Trans.) Stanford, California: Stanford University Press (Original work published 1987).

Rancière, Jacques (1995). *On the Shore of Politics*. (Liz Heron, Trans.) Londra, New York: Verso Press.

Rancière, Jacques (1994). *The Names of History: On the Poetics of Knowledge*. (Hassan Melehy, Trans.) Minneapolis, London: University of Minnesota Press (Original work published 1992).